"An exciting account"
—Best Sellers

"Stirring and suspense-filled . . . The author 'tells it like it was' and some portions include strong stuff, graphically portrayed and unfortunately true; the stuff that reawakens old nightmares for readers who participated long ago. The courage, suffering, mistakes and triumphs are all there in detail."

—Daily Press, Newport News

Edwin P. Hoyt is an eminent authority on naval history and, as biographer, historian, and novelist, has written more than eighty books, many of them recognized as among the best accounts ever written about men at war. Recent books of his include *The Battle of Leyte Gulf, How They Won the War in the Pacific, Nimitz and His Admirals, The Mutiny on the Globe, The Terrible Voyage,* and *Old Ironsides.* He is a former Army Air Corps flyer in WWII, a war correspondent and television producer. Mr. Hoyt now devotes his full time to writing books in his old sea captain's mansion on Nantucket Island, off the coast of Massachusetts.

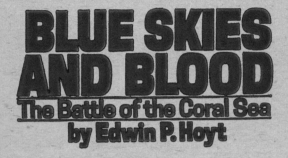

BLUE SKIES AND BLOOD

The Battle of the Coral Sea
by Edwin P. Hoyt

PINNACLE BOOKS   NEW YORK CITY

For Admiral Arleigh Burke

BLUE SKIES AND BLOOD

Copyright © 1975 by Edwin P. Hoyt

A Pinnacle Books edition, published by special arrangement with Paul S. Eriksson, Inc.

ISBN: 0-523-00907-0

First printing, September 1976

Cover illustration by Ed Valigursky

Printed in the United States of America

PINNACLE BOOKS, INC.
275 Madison Avenue
New York, N. Y. 10016

CONTENTS

Blue Skies and Blood

Introduction

Happy the nation that understands and wisely builds Seapower. From earliest times it has played a dominant role in world destiny. This role has advanced a few times in giant strides through developments that have changed the whole character of warfare.

This latest of E. P. Hoyt's stirring and suspense-filled books deals with one of these—the integration of the airplane into the fleet. Or rather, it deals with the dramatic manifestation in battle of this revolution in naval warfare that has forever affected the lives of all men.

The Battle of the Coral Sea occupies a unique niche in history. In these warm and distant waters for the first time the airplane afloat and not the big gun delivered the offensive blows on each side. Mighty fleets bitterly contested control of the sea far out of sight of their commanders.

Ever since man ventured afloat he has sought longer reach to injure the foe. The first significant extension came in the Middle Ages with the introduction of black powder and the big gun. However, ranges remained almost point blank in most battles until the Twentieth Century. Then the exploding Industrial Revolution made possible fire control equipment of increasing complexity and precision. The range of fleet action stretched out rapidly to as much as fifteen miles—over the horizon for the men at the guns.

Simultaneously the airplane came on the stage. It brought a Jove-like reach in range that far outshadowed the gun. In the 1920s extremists claimed that this new weapon with giant reach had done away with navies. Many believed and supported them. Fortunate for America that wiser men defeated their counsel and integrated the plane into the fleet.

Instead of doing away with navies, the wings in the sky brought phenomenal new powers. What calamity would have befallen the United States without a navy in World War II—and without aircraft carriers operating as an integral part of it.

The new potential in striking effectiveness was demonstrated at Pearl Harbor and elsewhere. But at Coral Sea for the first time carriers fought carriers. It was a break with the past, the unveiling of a new era in naval warfare comparable in its effect on fleet action to *Monitor-Virginia* (*Merrimack*) the duel that affected all naval warfare to come.

Coral Sea was also a turning point in the war. Here for the first time the "resistless" Japanese outward drive behind the spearhead of carrier task forces was blunted. By May, 1942 Japanese carrier pilots were combat veterans flushed with repeated victories. They seemed uncheckable.

So this significant battle doubly merits the talents of Mr. Hoyt. Diligent in research and fluent in writing, he skillfully unfolds the struggle in the Coral Sea through the lives and words of the participants. No fiction could surpass the heroism of many of those engaged, told in the laconic language of seamen accustomed to facing danger and the awesome strength of the sea. No epic could grip one more than the unadorned last words on voice radio between Commander Ault, *Lexington* Air Group Commander, and his unseen ship as he went to face his Maker alone in the vast and trackless sea.

American pilots and the ship crews though well trained lacked battle experience and the prestige of victory of the Japanese. An untried force meeting veterans has mountainous handicaps to overcome. Furthermore, the Japanese had a larger fleet than the U. S.

in the Pacific, partly through the government's lack of foresight and parsimony during the 1930s.

Historians have generally agreed that the Japanese gained a tactical victory at Coral Sea, since they suffered less *immediate* loss. But strategically the Americans came out far ahead. To my mind, they also did tactically. The foe's drive south had collapsed—just as a wave breaks and falls back from a towering cliff. The aura of invincible power had been shattered. A few thousand American sailors had gallantly met the challenge and greatly served the case of freedom.

More important tactical results of the battle would reach into the future to America's invaluable gain and Japan's disaster. Two of Japan's finest carriers, *Shokaku* and *Zuikaku*, were licking their battle wounds at home during the Battle of Midway. Had these veterans been present, it seems inevitable that Admiral Yamamotu would have won and, fatally for our times, changed the whole course of events to come.

Thus Coral Sea merits Mr. Hoyt's skilled narration that well brings out the far reaching effect of seapower upon the destiny of nations.

The influence of strength at sea has not declined since this historic battle. Instead it has grown. Thus Americans should mourn that so many of their representatives in Congress seem ready to allow the U. S. Navy to sink to inferiority.

Consequently the saga of the United States and liberty are imperiled as never before. Only by holding the sea can both survive. Without power there when the chips are down, all other power is futile. May this sound book help show Americans what strength afloat means to them. And may God grant us wisdom to spare no toil or sacrifice to regain supremacy before too late—and the hour is very late.

—Ernest M. Eller
Rear Admiral, USN. (Ret.)

Prologue

Sergeant Kawakami of Uchino Butai of the Imperial Japanese Army stood at the rail of the *Heian Maru*, and watched the low-lying shore of Japan recede in the distance. It was January 18, the Greater East Asia war had been going on for six weeks, and the results had been gratifying, if astounding to all Japanese. Radio Tokyo and the press had warned at the outset that Japan must expect a long and difficult struggle if she was to survive in the face of her powerful enemies—but those enemies had proved to be paper tigers, and the Imperial forces were victorious everywhere.

Just before midnight, the ship sailed in convoy for Camranh Bay, Indo-China, to await even more ships. Sergeant Kawakami now learned that he was to be a part of the force that would occupy the Dutch East Indies.

On February 10 the ships lay at anchor, swaying idly in the warm Southeast Asian sun. Eight days later a convoy of 70 transports, escorted by 30 warships, sailed for the East Indies. On March 1 the force landed after a brief naval battle with Dutch defenders, who were overwhelmed. Less than three weeks later the fighting had ended and the Japanese were mopping up, so secure that on March 20 General Imamura took time to hold a solemn memorial service for the noble Japanese soldiers killed in the battle for the occupation. Sergeant Kawakami held his men at attention in the clearing west of Army headquarters, while his superiors spoke sadly of their dead comrades.

In April, Sergeant Kawakami and his men were put to work guarding thousands of Dutch and British prisoners captured in the brief campaign, and the Indonesians and Chinese who were suspected of helping the westerners. He was attracted to some of them, particularly the children, but was warned sternly not to fraternize, for the prisoners were deadly enemies. As a loyal servant of his Imperial Majesty, Sergeant Kawakami never thought of disobeying.

Mid-April saw a change; the Japanese constructed permanent stockades, and separated the prisoners into compounds at Bandoeng, according to race. All was going remarkably well; Japan seemed to have no troubles at all, save administration in these unfamiliar areas.

The first little sign of trouble came on April 20, when Sergeant Kawakami learned from the news broadcasts that American planes had bombed Nagoya, Wakayama, and Tokyo in the homeland. The shock was immense, with the victories sustained it was hard to see how the Americans could launch such an offensive, and the tension in the camp at Bandoeng grew.

For several weeks prisoners had been escaping, but since the Japanese were everywhere most of them were recaptured or gave themselves up when the people refused to help them or were afraid to defy the Japanese army. In the past escaped prisoners had been scolded and returned to the stockade. But now it was different. Sergeant Kawakami and his comrades looked with new eyes on these western enemies:

In the evening at supper time the road leading to the west side of the second outpost was so crowded with visitors that it was hardly passable. Most of them were wives. Some had gained vantage points from where they could see better and were waving their hands; others even threw goods into the stockade. If it were our army the wives would feel ashamed; they would look down on their own husbands and probably could not face anyone. It must be the difference in races. That is the reason they surrendered without fighting.

Casual acceptance and toleration was now replaced with hostility. The enemy must be taught. So on April 22 when several prisoners were found to have escaped a unit of thirty soldiers was sent after them. Three were captured in the night and brought back. Next day at noon the three were killed by stabbing as a warning to the rest.

Sergeant Kawakami and his men watched their officers as the cruelty increased. On the day after the Emperor's birthday, another sergeant watched as officers brutalized prisoners, striking them on the head, gouging and twisting their arms, and that soldier was moved to write:

> When I think about the prisoners, I keenly feel that we must not lose the war. . . .

But there seemed no chance at all of losing the war, when one examined it from Sergeant Kawakami's position. The war, as Radio Tokyo told them, was virtually won. All the objectives had been taken; there remained only to extend the empire to its fullest, and destroy the remnants of the American fleet. Sergeant Kawakami and his men were sure the leaders of the army and the navy were now planning to do precisely that. Everywhere, in the Philippines, in Malaya, and south toward Australia the Japanese forces were in motion. A month earlier had come a report that the Japanese army had landed in New Zealand. No matter that it was premature—it was only a matter of time, Sergeant Kawakami and the others knew. In the south as elsewhere, Imperial soldiers and sailors were extending the perimeters of empire.

Chapter One

The Sun Still Rising

On the morning of April 7, 1942, Lieutenant Kiyoshige Sato of the Imperial Japanese Army left Rabaul
aboard the Japanese destroyer *Soya* on a special and
very important mission. *Soya*, in company with the
little Minesweeper Number 20, was to mop up retreating elements of the allied armies, and make sure
that no wireless stations were left in the interior of
New Britain island around the community of Talasea.
In a few days, the army and navy would launch an
amphibious assault from Rabaul against Port Moresby
and the Solomon islands—the next step in the neutrali-
zation and perhaps occupation of Australia. No word
of this move must reach the westerners. The mission-
aries and the planters, and above all any pockets of
soldiers who had reached this southern point after the
disasters in Malaya and the Dutch East Indies, must
be captured and quieted. So, Lieutenant Sato's mission was regarded as primary by his superiors.

Everything was being rushed these hectic days. After the strike at Pearl Harbor, in the Philippines, and
Malaya and the Indies, the Imperial Army had moved
with such flawless success and such ridiculous ease
that progress had surprised even the Imperial General
Staff in Tokyo. The Europeans seemed to vanish before the flag of the Rising Sun as frightened little fish
before a great shark. The easy captures of Singapore,

5

Hong Kong, the overrunning of the Philippines and Java and Sumatra, and above all the crippling of the fleets and military defenses of the westerners, had brought a wave of euphoria that convinced the Imperial Army of its absolute supremacy in the field. The war of expansion would be long and hard and dangerous said those who knew the west. Admiral Isoroku Yamamoto, chief of the combined fleet of the Imperial Navy, had long spoken out in high councils against such a war, but he had been overruled by the army, whose generals spoke of conquering all the Pacific, and perhaps even more. There was a military term for it: *hakko ichiu*—to bring all the corners of the world under one roof. Now the term seemed no longer poetic, but very possible.

Talasea sat in the middle of a long, narrow peninsula that jutted out from the center of New Britain island north, and was a natural landing place for soldiers fleeing from the islands already occupied and pacified. For years the Australians had maintained communications with such outlying areas by radio, and so there were known to be a number of wireless stations on the peninsula, and they must be quieted.

All this, Lieutenant Sato explained to Lieutenant Kakuo Shiometsu and Sergeant Takemitsu Hasegawa, and the thirty-five men under their command, as the ships steamed toward the peninsula. Their specific mission was to mop up enemy remnants in the Talasea area, occupy the wireless station there in the district governor's headquarters, and destroy all communications equipment. He did not explain matters of high strategy, for if he knew anything about the coming invasion of Port Moresby it was only wild rumor. He was not supposed to know, even though the plans in general had been drawn back in 1938 for just such a move. No one, not even the General Staff, had ex-

6

pected that the demand for this invasion would come so quickly. When war began it was assumed that it would take five or six months to conquer Malaya and the Philippines, but it had come so easily that the perimeter of the Japanese empire was to be pushed over the Coral Sea, and in the next few weeks.

Thus, just after dawn on the morning of April 8, Lieutenant Sato led his men ashore in a blinding tropical rainstorm and advanced into Talasea, where he set up a signal station for communication with air units that might be needed to make strikes in the jungle.

In half an hour the scouts reported that they had visited the four houses in the community, and that all, including the shop of a Chinese merchant, were empty. Just outside the port area, Sergeant Hasegawa entered the church, and found there a German missionary named Father Bernhard Franke and fifteen New Britain natives, but no enemy. The missionary offered to guide them and assured them there were no Australians or others in the vicinity.

Two hours later the Japanese had searched themselves, checked the old hospital and the houses of five Australians and found them all gone. They gave a stern warning to the German missionary, that he must submit himself wholeheartedly to the direction of the Imperial Japanese Army, and they left next day for other regions, to make the same kind of search. For two weeks Lieutenant Sato and his men scoured the area of central New Britain, and then came back to Rabaul to report that all was secure.

They found Rabaul a hive of activity. Early in March the Fourth Japanese fleet had occupied the towns of Lae and Salamaua in New Guinea, but the occupation of Port Moresby, a much larger place, had been delayed because of the presence or suspected

7

presence of American carriers. Imperial Headquarters now planned to take Port Moresby, the big Australian air base, and Tulagi in the Solomon Islands, where a sea plane base would be built. This invasion would give Japan control of the Coral Sea and easy access to Northern Australia, which could be observed at will to check on the allied buildup there.

Through March and now April, the Japanese had waited. They had ships, and naval vessels, but they were short of carriers. Early in the year the carriers had been operating in the Indian Ocean, attacking the British at Trincomalee and neutralizing their naval power there. In April the vast majority of the flattops were committed to the coming battle for Midway, where the American fleet was to be drawn out and destroyed.

But by mid-April the plans were made for the invasion of Port Moresby on May 10, using the Army's South Sea Detachment. Lieutenant Sato and his men quite probably would go into action once again. The army troops would be escorted by the Fourth Fleet and units of the Combined Fleet, including the Fifth Carrier Division, which meant the big carriers *Shokaku* and *Zuikaku*, which had participated in the raid on Pearl Harbor.

In mid-April, Vice Admiral Shigeyoshi Inouye moved his Fourth Fleet headquarters down from Truk to Rabaul to be close to the action. The big carriers were sent to Truk to pick up warplanes and bring them down to Rabaul, so they could give air protection on a round-the-clock basis to the landings in New Guinea and the Solomons.

On April 30, Japanese intelligence officers presented Admiral Inouye with their most up-to-date information about the enemy. The Americans, they said, had some 200 first-line fighter planes in Australia, concentrated in the Port Darwin and Townsville areas. Somewhere there was a small task force—probably one carrier. The British navy seemed to have sent out a force led by one battleship, with three or four cruisers and some destroyers.

A few enemy submarines seemed to be operating in the Bismarck Archipelago's waters, but what was there to fear? Japan had gone through five months of war losing only a handful of ships, and nothing larger than a destroyer among the naval vessels.

But one thing was apparent—the Americans were getting much better at reconaissance by air, and so concealment of the plan to attack Port Moresby was difficult, even if wireless stations on land had been knocked out by Lieutenant Sato and units like his.

That night the invasion force shoved off from Rabaul, headed for Tulagi in the Solomons, the first point of the invasion. The Port Moresby force was getting ready to move out from Truk.

The Japanese officers in command of this invasion were capable and experienced men. Admiral Inouye was characterized by American naval intelligence as "an exceptionally brilliant and capable officer." Before the war they had considered him to be pro-American, although of course in 1942 that appraisal was meaningless, because Admiral Inouye was a loyal servant of his emperor. He was fifty-three years old, a graduate of the Japanese naval academy in the class of 1909 who had risen rapidly; twenty years later he was a captain, in 1935 he had been appointed rear admiral. He was a highly experienced officer; he had served with the staff in Tokyo, he had been chief of staff to the China Area Fleet in the war against Chiang Kai-shek's Nationalist government; he had been head of Japanese naval aviation, and for a time director of the Naval Academy. Inouye came from a long and distinguished line; his father was a samurai. One brother was a high official of the Mitsubishi combine; another brother was a lieutenant general in the army; still another was President of the Miyasaki gas company. Inouye was, then, competent, loyal, high-placed, and a nobleman with a grand stake in the strength of Japan.

The Port Moresby attack was called Operation MO, and for this work Admiral Inouye had assembled as strong a force as could be given him, considering the launching of the great armada against Midway. The landbased air force, which was being ferried south from Truk in part, consisted of about 150 planes under Rear Admiral Sadayoshi Yamada. The carrier striking force under Vice Admiral Takeo Takagi, consisted of heavy cruisers *Myoko*, and *Haguro*, six destroyers, an oiler and the two big carriers. Rear Admiral Tadaichi Hara commanded this force.

Then came the invasion force under Rear Admiral Aritomo Goto, whose flagship was the cruiser *Aoba*. The invaders of Tulagi rode in a transport, and were covered by a pair of minelayers and two destroyers and several smaller ships. No real trouble was expected at Tulagi. The Port Moresby invasion force was much larger. Rear Admiral Sadamichi Kajioka led six destroyers, which covered eleven transports, a number of converted minesweepers, two oilers and a repair ship, plus a minelayer and a minesweeper, and they were protected by a pair of light cruisers, a seaplane carrier, three gunboats and Admiral Goto with four cruisers and the light carrier *Shoho*. This last ship was an old one, her hull converted for air use. She displaced 12,000 tons, and could make only 25 knots—which meant she could not keep up with the larger carriers of 20,000 tons and more that could make 30 knots. Thus the kind of job she was assigned to do here was just right for her.

On April 30, as the Japanese units began moving according to the complicated schedule that would bring transports and their covering ships to the proper places at the proper times, the plan was for invasion of Tulagi on May 3, and then invasion of Port Moresby by the much larger force on May 10.

On May 1, the Australians, who knew that something was happening in the Solomons and that a Japanese force was at sea, withdrew the small garrison and civil officials from Tulagi, which was the headquarters of the island protectorate. And so two days later, when the Japanese arrived on the sandy coral beach, there was not the slightest opposition to their landing. The cruisers and destroyers and the carrier *Shoho* were offshore, waiting to support the operation with attacks on any allied naval units that might come by—but no real attack was expected. The big carriers *Shokaku* and *Zuikaku* were still busy, carrying more planes from Truk to Rabaul to support the coming operation against Port Moresby, where it was expected there really would be a fight.

So as darkness fell at Tulagi, the Japanese were settling in, getting ready to build a seaplane base for the future. Construction troops brought their equipment ashore, and seaplanes rode at buoys in the protected harbor. To the northeast, that night, Admiral Kajioka's Port Moresby invasion group moved out from Rabaul, headed at a leisurely safe pace for Port Moresby. All was quiet; another of the succession of Japanese easy victories seemed to be in the making.

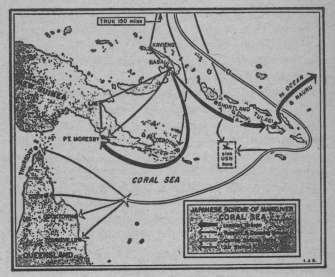

Japanese Scheme of Maneuver

Chapter Two

Intelligence

In the spring of 1942, the Americans knew a good deal more about Japanese dispositions and intentions than the men of the Rising Sun might have suspected. Lulled by the ease with which they had made their conquests, the Japanese, and the Japanese army in particular, tended to become contemptuous of the weakling westerners. As Sergeant Kawakami found it hard to understand the lack of the Bushido spirit among the Dutch and Indonesian prisoners he saw, so senior Japanese officers convinced themselves that the decadent colonial powers would be unable to fight, and were totally ill-equipped to meet the Japanese juggernaut. There were wiser heads among the Japanese leaders but had those wiser heads (such as Admiral Yamamoto,) had their way, there would have been no Pearl Harbor and no war at all.

Although battered and retreating everywhere, the allies of the English-speaking world were far from defeated. If their military machinery had been creaky at the beginning of the war—at least their intelligence organizations were functioning. At Pearl Harbor, Admiral Nimitz and his staff had a very good idea of what the Japanese were doing, particularly after the occupation of Lae and Salamaua on the long tip of New Guinea.

The Americans knew that Rabaul, on the northern

tip of New Britain island, was going to be a very important place. Before the war even few navy men had paid much attention to New Britain, or the Bismarck Sea or the long string of islands known as the Solomons which extend southeastward, overhanging Austrialia. But in March, 1942, they knew a good deal. Rabaul had suddenly become an important place, the concentration point for Japanese shipping. Japanese transports and warships came in to moor at the wharves on the northeast side of the harbor, or to anchor out in Simpson harbor. There were seaplane moorings and a beaching ramp between the town and Sulphur Creek. The whole sleepy area had been militarized and fortified in the few weeks since the Japanese took over. At Lakunai airdrome, the Japanese now had a dozen fighters and twenty bombers. They were building a new landing field at West Foresdore. The whole area was protected by anti-aircraft batteries at Government House, north of the Main Wharf, on Observatory Hill and at the Burns Phillip pier. Other anti-aircraft batteries were scattered around the 1000 foot hills, along the route southwest which led to Vanakanau aerodrome, where more fighters and bombers were stationed. From Rabaul, the Japanese patrol planes searched out six hundred miles for allied craft, which took them very near Australia, but not quite. What they needed was a base on one of the string of Solomons closer to the continent.

New Ireland, Buka, and Watom island were Japanese bases. The Imperial forces were also known to have occupied Kieta, in the Solomons, which had an aerodrome. But the field was not suitable for military operations, so it was really no good to them.

The advance Japanese bases were at Lae and Salamaua, ports with deep water anchorage. Lae was important for its big airfield, which had been used by the Australians before. It was a strong base, with an estimated 30 fighters and 15 bombers and a number of patrol planes.

The Australian coastwatchers had been on the job, and by this time they had the Japanese well under watch. They knew the routine plane procedure at Lae for search missions. The planes warmed up at 0530, took off 45 minutes later, and then began patrols that lasted from 0630 until 1815, operating at 5000 to 8000 feet altitude. But on days with bad visibility no planes were sent off at all.

The Americans also knew that the Japanese were moving air power down from the Marianas and the Marshall islands. And, even in March they could say that air attacks on Port Moresby and Tulagi indicated that the Japanese had plans for those places.

Indeed, everything pointed that way. The Japanese were massing shipping at Rabaul. Some twenty cargo and transports were in the area, far too many for re-supply of small bases. There were not very many warships in the Rabaul area, but that was not to be expected. The navy moved to targets, and did not send out calling cards. A submarine tender was sitting in Rabaul harbor, and three or four submarines were operating in the area. An occasional aircraft carrier showed up, ferrying planes. Occasionally a light cruiser called at Simpson harbor, and Destroyer Squadron Six operated out of there, along with Gunboat Division 8. *Kamikawa Maru* and *Fujikawa Maru*, two seaplane tenders, were in harbor there, which meant an unusual concentration of a particular kind of strength.

All signs pointed to a major military operation to begin from the Rabaul area around the first of May. The Japanese army had concentrated strength at Truk and Palao, and the Truk units had been moved out. At least one big convoy was known to be coming to the New Britain area.

As for Japanese naval strength that might be in the area, Nimitz knew that the carriers *Zuikaku* and *Shokaku* were located either in Truk or heading south, and the carrier *Ryukaku* was also in the area, operating independently. They could spot three heavy cruisers and at least seventeen destroyers in these waters.

To contest them, the Americans were already moving. They had sent 22,000 Army troops to Noumea in New Caledonia, and several Army Air Corps pursuit squadrons were flying out of the base. The seaplane carrier *Tangier* and twelve big flying boats were stationed there.

Efate in the New Hebrides was occupied as a base. Several New Zealand warships were stationed at Efate, and a handful of American destroyers. Americans were heading for Tonga, in four big transports to set up a base. If the Japanese were up to something more in the South Pacific, the Americans were getting ready to contest their passage.

Chapter Three

Clouds Over Pearl Harbor

At Pearl Harbor in mid-April, Admiral Chester Nimitz was very much worried over several recent developments. He knew that something was cooking in the Central Pacific. His intelligence officers had broken the Japanese naval code, and were reading messages that indicated the enemy was moving in force against Midway—at least they were fairly sure the code name meant Midway. Also, Admiral King had usurped Admiral Halsey and the carriers *Enterprise* and *Hornet* for the raid of Lieutenant Colonel Jimmy Doolittle and his flock of B-25 medium bombers on Japan. This left two carrier task forces for use in the Pacific—Rear Admiral Frank Jack Fletcher's Task Force 17, which was operating out of Noumea in New Caledonia, and centered on the carrier *Yorktown*; and Rear Admiral Aubrey Fitch's Task Force 11, with carrier *Lexington* which was just then in Pearl Harbor for upkeep.

All the new Japanese movement around Tulagi, Rabaul, and Truk had not gone unobserved by Australians and others. General Douglas MacArthur's intelligence units in Australia were keeping Nimitz and his staff informed, for MacArthur had a huge stake in the safety of Port Moresby, it figured large in his plans for movement back up the island chains to the Philippines as soon as he had the strength. Toward the end of April, then, as the Japanese massed their forces in Truk and Rabaul for the movement to New Guinea's southeast shore, they were seen, and their intentions were very generally understood. Nimitz was warned and took every precaution to forestall them.

The Japanese had anticipated that they would have some kind of naval battle before the Port Moresby landing was finished. Their intelligence showed one American carrier in the area—which was accurate enough, even if they thought it was *Saratoga*, when actually it was Fletcher's *Yorktown*. The Japanese also knew of the land-based air force in Australia, and that was the reason for the heavy movement of their own land-based air from Truk to Rabaul. Admiral Inouye planned to entice the American naval units into the Coral Sea, and there to catch them in a pincers between Admiral Goto with light carrier *Shoho* and his cruisers on the one side, and Admiral Takeo Takagi, with his two fleet carriers, cruisers and destroyers on the other.

But Nimitz, even with relatively small forces at his disposal at the moment, was not to be caught napping thus. Admiral Fitch and *Lexington* was told to rendezvous with Fletcher west of the New Hebrides islands, and be prepared for action. Nimitz also ordered up whatever MacArthur could give him from the Anzac command, which was becoming MacArthur's navy just then. MacArthur had Rear Admiral J.G. Crace of the Royal Navy and several cruisers. To these were added the American cruiser *Chicago* and the destroyer *Perkins*, which were in the area. So the Americans were able to put forth a small but still respectable force to meet the Japanese threat. If fate would wait a little they could do better. Admiral Halsey and his two carriers were due in any day from

18

the Tokyo raid and could get moving on short notice. But Nimitz could not wait and hope—he had to act.

On April 25 Nimitz was in San Francisco, meeting with Admiral King, and listening to King complain that he was not at all pleased with Admiral Fletcher's performance of carrier warfare over the past few weeks. Fletcher, said Admiral King, did not seem to be aggressive enough to carry the war against the enemy. Nimitz, the great pacifier, agreed that Fletcher's conduct so far had not been aggressive. But since he had no time to make a change at the moment, and no better prospect for command in sight, they agreed to wait and see what Fletcher did in the near future before making a final decision as to his fate.

Returning to Pearl Harbor and assessing the intelligence reports of the last few days, Nimitz knew that something was going to happen down in the South Pacific almost momentarily. *Shoho* and her accompanying warships had been spotted in the area, and the presence of the two big carriers was also known. Further, the Australians had plenty of evidence of the movement of various transports into the Rabaul area, and so something big was definitely afoot. If it could only wait for Halsey. But . . .

Halsey, with Task Force 16, was told almost as soon as he pulled into port from the Tokyo raid that he was to take his carrier down to the South Pacific, sailing on April 30, and take command of operations down there. But Nimitz knew almost for certain that Halsey would never arrive in time, and that he must depend on Frank Jack Fletcher.

Neither Nimitz at Pearl Harbor nor King in Washington had too much confidence. Fletcher's way of fighting the war was not theirs. By now he might have put a serious crimp in the Japanese plans to strike at Port Moresby by attacking Rabaul and its naval facilities with his carrier planes. But Fletcher had the feeling that if he attacked Rabaul that would let the enemy know where he was, and that was not a good idea. He was waiting for the Japanese navy to bring the battle to him. For a month he had been moving around the area, arriving a little late each time he planned a raid. He was going to raid the Shortland Islands on April 6, and when he got there the Japanese had left. He was going to make another raid, but a week later he became worried about operational troubles and supply shortages, and so went into port at Togatubu to solve his problems. Nimitz hoped he would be ready and able to fight when the moment came. He had to depend on Fletcher.

As the Japanese slipped out of Truk and Rabaul and headed south, in Pearl Harbor Nimitz and his staff were finishing up their plan of battle, having guessed just about what Inouye and his men were up to. On April 30 the plan was radioed to Admiral Fletcher—he was to take his force, and with it Admiral Fitch's force and Admiral Crace's force, and to operate in the Coral Sea beginning May 1. Nimitz had no doubt that Fletcher would find a battle here.

Admiral Fletcher, facing almost certain battle that might prove decisive, immediately put his staff to work laying a battle plan.

This admiral, pink and brown in the face, with bright eyes overshadowed by heavy brows that had looked long into the ocean sun, was a deep-sea sailor, whose experience from the beginning had been in ships——big ships——battleships and cruisers, for the most part. He was experienced, a graduate of the Naval Academy and of the U.S. Naval War College and the Army War College. He had served as aide to Secretary of the Navy Swanson for a time, and for a time on the staff in Washington. When the Japanese attacked Pearl Harbor, Fletcher was commander of Cruiser Division Six of the U.S. Fleet, and in the spring of 1942 his basic assignment was as Commander of Cruisers of the Pacific Fleet. To him an aircraft carrier was primarily a ship which carried airplanes but was still to be managed as a ship. He was very strong on traditional naval techniques. Fuelling and provisionment were much on his mind at all times, and needed to be done properly, under proper conditions. When the task forces of Admiral Fitch and Admiral Crace joined up with Admiral Fletcher on May 1, the first thought that crossed Fletcher's mind was the need to fuel and thus be ready for action when it might come. So the ships assembled and stood by for fuelling. Fletcher estimated it would take about four days for the whole force.

The Japanese, however, were not waiting four days for the Americans to fuel. On May 2 came the word from MacArthur that the enemy was moving. Fletcher broke away, leaving Fitch and his force still fuelling, and steamed in toward the Solomons to see what he could do. By the morning of May 3 he was in the middle of the Coral Sea, and ready if something happened. He was fuelling again. His destroyers were standing by the oiler *Neosho* and topping off, one after the other, even as the Japanese soldiers in their gray green tropical uniforms, piled through the surf to the beach at Tulagi.

News of that invasion did not reach Fletcher. He sent oiler *Neosho* to the rendezvous point where he had planned to meet Admiral Fitch's force. Fletcher refused to break radio silence, so *Neosho* carried the word that he had gone on ahead to a point which Fitch and Crace should make at daybreak on May 5. The point was three hundred miles south of Guadalcanal island. Fletcher was now, at long last ready to do battle. He was preparing to strike Tulagi.

The Japanese had begun to relax after landing their forces so easily at Tulagi The Australians had deserted the place, and obviously there were no Americans here. About two hours after the landing was secure the Japanese covering force turned around and headed back for the open sea. The transports unloaded with no pressure at all, and began drifting off to join their escorts. By dark most of the ships were gone from the area. Radio reports of the ease of the operation reached Admiral Takagi and Admiral Hara, who were in command of the heavy ships supporting the whole MO Operation. They saw no reason to hurry or change their plans. *Zuikaku* and *Shokaku* flew off the last of the planes ferried down from Truk, and their officers prepared to turn their attention to the coming Port Moresby invasion, where that allied opposition was definitely expected.

At 1900, the news of the Tulagi landing hit Fletcher's flagship like a bomb. The word came in from Australia that air search planes had spotted Japanese landing ships and transports off Tulagi. The enemy had taken another bit of territory, this one far too close to Australia for comfort. Fletcher was going to have to do something about it, alone, and immediately. The course he set was carrying him to a point 100 miles off Guadalcanal, while Fitch and Crace heading for the rendezvous point, were heading the other way. The American force was badly fragmented and quite unready for any serious Japanese opposition.

Fletcher was very nervous. He regarded the carrier as a weapon valuable when it could be used in surprise and tremendously vulnerable otherwise. The loss of surprise was to him the worst thing that might happen in a battle. Thus the day before, when a scout plane sighted a Japanese submarine on the surface, Fletcher was concerned lest his presence be known to the enemy. He sent three planes after the sub. They located the submarine, bombed it, but returned without definite news of a kill, and Fletcher worried more because for the first time in two months the Japanese might now know where he was in the area.

Yet he was very lucky. That night as the eleven ships of his task force changed course and headed for the Solomons, they ran into foul weather, which masked their presence. Ten minutes before sunrise the *Yorktown* began launching planes. Lieutenant Commander Oscar Pederson, leader of *Yorktown*'s air group stayed aboard the ship, grounded so that he could serve as fighter director as the planes moved out.

Yorktown was moving easily at 23 knots, head into the wind. The weather was not what the pilots would have ordered: rain squalls and winds of up to 35 knots which made it hard to estimate flying speed and capability, and hard even to take off from the carrier.

The first planes off the deck were six fighters of VF-42, whose commander was Lieutenant Commander C.R. Fenton, an Annapolis boy who had graduated from the Naval Academy in 1929 and who elected to become a naval aviator two years later. Those first six fighters would set up the combat air patrol, to circle around the carrier and her support ships, protecting them from any incursions by enemy planes.

Then came the strike force, thirteen dive bombers led by Lieutenant Commander W. O. Burch, and fifteen others led by Lieutenant W. C. Short. Burch's planes were the scouting force, armed with 1000-pound bombs. Short's were also thus armed, but they were not given the additional duty of moving out ahead and finding the target. Burch sped ahead.

Behind these came twelve of the old slow TBD Torpedo Bombers, each carrying a Mark 13 torpedo. They flew alone, for *Yorktown*'s fighters had been having trouble with the self-sealing aspect of their gastanks, and on this day Admiral Fletcher ordered that almost all the fighters be kept back at the carrier to take turns at combat air patrol.

Early in the morning then, the American planes were heading toward the Solomon islands, flying through heavy cloud cover and rain squalls, wondering if they would ever see the enemy from their vantage point of 17,000 feet. They had trouble keeping together, or sending information to the other forces because their radios were not working well; the static was heavy and the voices were indistinct. But they moved on through the gusts.

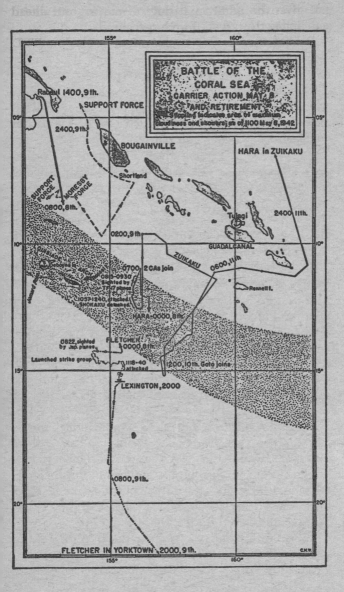

BATTLE OF THE
CORAL SEA
CARRIER ACTION MAY 8
AND RETIREMENT
Stippling indicates area of maximum
cloudiness and showers, as of 1100 May 8, 1942.

Rabaul 1400, 9th.

SUPPORT FORCE

2400, 9th.

BOUGAINVILLE

Shortland

HARA in ZUIKAKU

SUPPORT FORCE

MORESBY FORCE

0800, 8th.

0200, 9th.

ZUIKAKU

Tulagi

2400, 11th.

GUADALCANAL

Rebaul in A.M.

0700, 2 CAs join

0600, 11th.

Rennell I.

085-0930
sighted by
TF-17 planes

1057-1240, sighted
SHOKAKU detached

HARA-0000, 8th.

0822, sighted
by Jap planes

FLETCHER
0000, 8th.

Launched strike group

1118-40
detached

1200, 10th. Goto joins

LEXINGTON, 2000

0800, 9th.

FLETCHER IN YORKTOWN, 2000, 9th.

C.H.W.

Chapter Four

Tulagi

On the morning of May 4 the sky over Tulagi harbor on Florida island was spotted with big white fleecy clouds. The sun skirted them and the weather was fine, the palms along the shoreline rustling in the ocean breeze. Two Japanese destroyers, the *Kikuzuki* and *Yutsuki* stood in close to shore at anchor.

Admiral Shima, in his flagship, the *Okinoshima*, had spent a quiet restful night, and was ready to get on with the work of establishing a seaplane base here. Four anti-aircraft guns and several machine guns had been moved ashore with the invasion force the day before and erected around the port. Men of the Seventh Construction Section and the Eighth Base Unit were already at work building facilities, and six seaplanes rode in the harbor, floating gently on the water.

At about 0830 Lieutenant Commander Burch looked down from his cockpit and saw a ship below, speeding away from West Cape of Guadalcanal, heading north, its graceful wake trailing out behind. He thought it was a destroyer, but there was no time to stop and take a second look; his job was to reach Tulagi and set up the attack.

Not quite fifteen minutes later the thirteen American scout bombers approached Tulagi, and there below, clearly visible through the clouds was a Japanese fleet. The eager Americans, not yet very experienced in the art of war, saw a cruiser, and two very large transports, plus three smaller ones, two destroyers, lying moored together, and four gunboats and various other small craft.

Lieutenant Commander Burch gave the signal, and they nosed over in their dive attack from 19,000 feet, moving to an angle of 70° when they hit 10,000 feet, and then holding steady until they dropped to 2500 feet, when the pilots pulled back on the stick, and the bomb shackles released the bombs.

Below, on the ground, the Japanese gunners manned their 8 centimeter anti-aircraft guns and the 13 millimeter machine guns, and a rain of white blossoms and spitting bullets came up toward the planes. The anti-aircraft gunners on the destroyers and the other ships opened up, But the Japanese gunners were inexperienced, and the heavy fire was inaccurate. No one was hit, Burch circled, attacking the "cruiser" and the two destroyers, and then headed home, to report four sure bomb hits and one probable.

Next to arrive over Tulagi were the twelve torpedo bombers, and Lieutenant Commander Joe Taylor led them in, swift and sure. Joe Taylor was in his element—he had wanted to be an aviator since the day he entered the naval academy in 1923. After graduation in June Week, 1927 he stayed on for a course in aviation, and joined the new carrier *Lexington* when she was commissioned that same December. More training, and he served with *Lexington* until the spring of 1931 when he was transferred to scouting planes at the shore base at Pearl Harbor, and then went to air duty with the cruiser *Astoria*. He had taken over Torpedo Squadron 5 in May, 1941 when the *Yorktown* was operating in the Atlantic and he

27

was experienced—had already led raids on the Gilberts and Marshalls and on Salamaua and Lae after the Japanese occupied those New Guinea towns.

Lieutenant Commander Taylor gave his orders quickly. Three of the planes were directed in on the nearest transport, seven went after the two destroyers, and what they thought was the "cruiser" moored nearby. But the destroyers were actually two small minesweepers, *Toshi Maru* and *Tama Maru*, and the cruiser was actually destroyer *Kikuzuki*.

The first attack on the transport failed. Two of the torpedoes blew up on the beach, hurting nothing but sending clouds of sand and spray into the jungle. The seven planes that went after the other ships dropped only six torpedoes; one excited pilot had forgotten to turn on his switch, so when he pushed it, the torpedo did not release. He flew back to *Yorktown* with the torpedo, landed, and learned to his chagrin the price of inexperience.

But the other six "fish" did their job well. *Tama Maru* began settling in the water and sank. Another, smaller minesweeper sank, too. And destroyer *Kikuzuki*, hit and holed, began to run for the beach.

Two other torpedo bombers attacked a transport, which was lying anchored and when they left they were sure they had sunk it.

As the American planes bored in, coming down to fifty feet above the water and moving to within five hundred yards of the ships before releasing, the Japanese gunners put up a spatter of fire, but no one was hit. The torpedo planes then headed back for the ship, and the second wave of divebombers swooped down.

Lieutenant Short had divided his force of fifteen planes into three sections. The first section attacked the same transport that the torpedo bombers had gone after, but got no hits at all, the closest miss being 30 feet away from the hull.

By this time, fifteen minutes after the beginning of the attack on Tulagi, the Japanese had fully recovered from the early confusion of surprise. One pilot swam out to his plane, anchored off Makambo Island in the bay, and managed to get the engine started. He revved up the propellor, sped along the surface, and the single big float made its wake boil as the plane lifted off. The plane was well-camouflaged, gray and brown to match the shadows of the jungle above the water, but the tell-tale orange suns on the wingtips left no doubt as to what she was, and the frustrated bomber pilots swooped down, strafed, and caught the slender seaplane just as she lifted. A shudder, a twist, and then the pilot slumped, the plane nosed over and crashed.

The second American division went after what they thought was a seaplane tender, but could not claim more than one possible hit. The third division attacked the same ship from a different angle—or started to. Three went in, scoring one hit and one possible, but the other two planes veered off and went after that big transport and one of the minesweepers—but missed.

Less than an hour after the attack began, the attack group was circling the carrier, waiting one by one to land, and as the tires skidded across the decks, the armorers were waiting, and the gas tanks were filled, the pilots made ready to man their planes again. Another hour, and the planes were ready and beginning to take off for the second strike.

Yorktown had been maneuvering to keep the wind in proper direction during takeoff and landing at nine knots, saving fuel, loafing along, waiting while her birds of prey did their lethal job.

This time the dive bombers took off first, fourteen of them. Less than half an hour later the scout bombers headed out, thirteen of them again. Last came the torpedo bombers, only eleven this time, as one of the planes was not ready to operate.

When Lieutenant Commander Burch's scout bombers reached the Solomons, this time the Japanese were in motion. The ships had begun to move out, heading north, back for Rabaul and safety. The transport was steaming out of Tulagi harbor, and one destroyer and several minesweepers were in motion. The bombers dived in, and were promptly attacked by one seaplane. The gunners tracked the elusive plane in their sights. It was fast and maneuvered well. But there were too many American planes, and only one Japanese plane, and in a few moments the seaplane was spinning down into the sea.

This time the anti-aircraft gunners aboard the ships under attack had recovered from surprise and were firing accurately. One dive bomber was hit. A shell put a ten-inch hole in the rudder and a twenty-inch hole in the right elevator. Another cut a three-inch piece out of the right horizontal stabilizer. But the Douglas plane was tough, and the pilot made it back to the carrier even with all that blue sky showing. A second plane was hit by small arms fire, perhaps the machine guns from Makambo island.

The inaccuracy of the bombing was partly due to fogging of the windshields of the dive bombers, so severe that most of the pilots could not use their bombsights, but had to drop more or less by guess. Some of the error was due to the fortunes of war, and some to pilot error. The torpedo bombers were not doing well at all—the first division on this second attack dropped six torpedoes, and not one of them connected. The planes did manage to chase a seaplane attacker back to Makambo Island, but he landed safely and the Americans were driven off by heavy, accurate AA fire. The second division of five planes went after that same transport, whose canny Japanese captain was maneuvering as if he was operating a speedboat instead of a ship, and the AA fire was so heavy that the planes dropped their torpedoes from 1500 yards out, and got no hits. They reformed, strafed a few launches and small craft in Tulagi harbor, and then flew back towards *Yorktown*. One torpedo bomber became separated from the others, and the pilot got lost in the cloud cover. He flew around until his gas ran out at 1606. The men of *Yorktown* knew because they could hear his radio transmissions right up to the moment he ditched. The trouble was that his receiver was not working, and no one could help him. So the plane went in, and although searches were made by air and sea, neither pilot nor crewman was ever found.

Lieutenant Commander Pederson sent the second strike of bombers out on a scouting mission of their own, northwest of Florida Island, to try to find Japanese ships that were fleeing Tulagi. Five planes closed on a gunboat and blew it out of the water. Five more went after a second gunboat, and did the same. The remaining four planes struck the leading gunboat, which was hit, and later beached near Vatilau island.

When Admiral Fletcher learned that there were fighter seaplanes in the harbor, he let go four of the fighters of the air cover group, and sent them off to knock out the seaplanes. They launched at 1340 and went looking. They found the planes, in the air and ready for battle, and shot down all three of them, then strafed ships in the harbor at Tulagi and headed back. Two of the fighters got lost in the clouds and

31

landed on the south coast of Guadalcanal island, near Cape Henslow. The planes had to be scratched, but the pilots were both safe and they were spotted on the beach.

The Americans were straining for action this day. A third strike was launched at 1430, and resulted in more hits on small craft and landing barges, but those bigger ships simply could not be sunk, it seemed. There were too many misses. Still, when the planes came back as dusk began to roll in over the horizon, the pilots were jubilant. They had met the enemy in open battle for the first time, and they believed they had sunk two destroyers, a freighter, four gunboats, beached a light cruiser, and damaged another destroyer, a freighter, and a seaplane tender.

All this time the Japanese at Tulagi had been shouting for help, but there was no one nearby to help them. Admiral Takagi, in charge of the big carriers, did not hear about the action until after noon, when he was off Bougainville. Then he was fueling, which prevented him from doing anything immediately. He sped south, but it was long after dark before he reached the same area where the Americans might be, and they were not there.

After dark, American destroyer *Hammann* was sent over to Guadalcanal to pick up those two downed fighter pilots. The Task Force was speeding south, to make rendezvous with Admiral Fitch and the *Lexington*. The men of *Yorktown* were jubilant, proud of themselves and their planes, and Captain Elliott Buckmaster of *Yorktown* proposed to recommend every pilot for a medal. After a long dry spell, punctuated by many humiliating defeats at the hands of the Japanese, the Americans felt they had scored a clean-cut victory.

Hammann headed in toward Cape Henslow at a

speed of 30 knots and at 1810 was off the coast of Guadalcanal, 2 miles from Cape Henslow, where the fliers were reported to have come down. At 1810, too, the ship was close enough to the beach that the lookouts could spot a white marker at the proper place, east of the cape. It was hard to see well, because darkness was falling, and they were running through rain squalls. But in a few minutes, from the bridge the searchers spotted the two planes, very close together, where they had crash landed.

It was tough going. The rain was pelting down in squalls, sometimes obscuring the beach totally from the men on the ship. But they knew the pilots were in there, and they discovered that the white marker was a parachute which the two pilots had made into a tent.

On the shore, Lieutenant (jg) E.S. McCuskey and Ensign J.P. Adams waved frantically as the destroyer came up, and they tried to launch their rubber boats into the surf, but were thrown back. The wind, and the waves were too much for them.

Meanwhile, the destroyer had slowed to a stop, and a motor whale boat was put over the side. Ensign R.P.F. Enright led a crew of six seamen, who moved out from the ship, six thousand yards out from the beach. The boat arrived 150 yards offshore just at dusk, but could not make a landing because of the heavy surf.

Was it stalemate?

Coxswain George Wilson Kapp, Jr. then volunteered to swim a line into shore, and he jumped over the side, and made his way through the hard breaking surf, sometimes almost totally obscured from his comrades, until he reached a point, half exhausted, where the fliers could grab him and pull him ashore.

All three were then pulled back through the surf to the boat.

There, after the pilots had begun expressing their thanks for the hand up, Ensign Enright asked them if they had been able to wreck their planes. They had tried, but they had not been able to do much damage, they said. Enright had been ordered to destroy both aircraft to prevent them from falling into Japanese hands, and now the sailors opened fire with rifles to try to set the gas tanks aflame, but they had no luck. Lieutenant McCuskey and Ensign Adams said they had destroyed the confidential gear, and their papers, but that was not enough. McCuskey then offered to go ashore again and burn the planes if possible, and Enright had brought along pyrotechnic material for just this purpose. So McCuskey started swimming in with a line. He ran into harsh breakers which swirled the line around him and nearly drowned him, so he threw it off. Then the line, slack, fouled in the boat's propellers, and the engine conked. The boat began drifting in towards the beach, the men paddling furiously to keep it out of the surf where it would capsize, while Boatswain's Mate Second Class Albert Stanley Jason leaped overboard and dived to clear the line from the propellers. He started to use a knife, then came back and got a hacksaw before he could finish the job.

McCuskey, after fighting the surf on the way in, collapsed on the beach, exhausted. He lay there on the beach, and in the gathering darkness the boat crew could not see him. For half an hour the crew waited, worrying, and wondering if the Japanese might have agents on the island. Then, by the light of a starshell from a Very pistol, one of the crew spotted McCuskey on the beach, and Kapp volunteered to swim in with a line again. He tried, but had to come back, defeated by surf and his own exhaustion. Jason then took the line and made the trip successfully. The two tried a few times to set the planes afire, but they were wet, and would not flame. Ensign Enright was getting nervous. The destroyer had been lying too quiet too long, in these dangerous waters, and they were, in a sense, bait for an enemy submarine if there was one around the area. So it was decided to abandon the destruction attempt, and Jason and McCuskey were hauled back through the surf by the line, and the boat headed for the *Hammann*. The whole effort had taken three hours, and had very nearly come a cropper. It would have failed had not Jason been able to make that last swim in to shore to save the tired McCuskey.

For the men of *Hammann* and all the task force, night had brought a satisfying end to a very busy day.

Chapter Five

Sparring

On the evening of May 4, at Bandoeng the Japanese had made the decision that all but' a handful of Japanese prisoners of war would be released. So well was the war going, so little had been the damage to the oil installations and the industrial plant of the Netherlands East Indies that Japan was nearly half a year ahead of the schedule set down in the months before the war began. The Greater East Asia Co-Prosperity Sphere was almost certain to be successful, said the economic planners. The best way to get it all going was to make friends with the people involved.

So Sergeant Kawakami and his men relaxed, and on the evening of May fourth their prisoners were told that most of them would be released the following morning. And next morning it was done, as Kawakami and his men stood by and watched:

From 0500 on their uniforms were inspected, and they were released from the front gate. Having been prisoners and not knowing whether they were going to live or die, they are suddenly released. They are able to return to their homes and to their work. How happy they are! Even though we cannot understand their tongue, their feelings are shown on their faces. We too are happy. We are praying that these people will become the nucleus which will build the new prosperous Java.

As the Javanese prisoners melted away along the roads that led to the villages and kampongs, a thousand miles to the southwest Admiral Fletcher's *Yorktown* force was meeting up with Admiral Fitch's *Lexington* group and Admiral Crace's support group. The rendezvous point was three hundred miles south of the Solomons. Destroyer *Hammann* had gone off alone to rescue the downed fighter pilots on Guadalcanal, and joined up this morning. Destroyer *Perkins* having searched all night for the survivors of the ditched torpedo bomber, gave up and joined the task force again. There was a report that the pilot and his crewman had made Guadalcanal, but it was not confirmed. There was also a report from an Australian coastwatcher that nine ships had been sunk in and around Tulagi harbor.

After steaming furiously all night, Admiral Takagi, with his eleven-ship force, reached a point about a hundred miles south of Santa Isabel island, in the middle of the Solomons. In the morning he took a look for the Americans, and a run by Tulagi to see what was happening there. Nothing at all was happening; the ships left in harbor were sunk or on the beach; the planes were sunk; the Tulagi force had been disbanded and the surviving ships had already gone to join the *MO* operation against Port Moresby.

Admiral Takagi suffered, at the moment, as did Admiral Fletcher, from a shortage of good air intelligence. Fletcher's problem was that while the Australians and General MacArthur were flying many missions daily from Australia and Port Moresby, the communications between the naval force and MacArthur left much to be desired. Takagi's problem was that while the Japanese maintained a careful and effective surveillance of these waters by four-engined flying boats, which had long range and sharp eyes, his communications were no better than Fletcher's. On the morning of May 5, just after the task forces joined up one of *Yorktown*'s patrol planes spotted a four-engined Kawanishi flying boat, and shot it down. Undoubtedly the pilot and crew radioed their position and a call for help, but since the flying boat was under the command of the 25th Air Flotilla at Rabaul, and not Admiral Inouye at that same place, the word was slow in getting to Inouye. Consequently he did not tell Takagi—and the two of them used their forces as they would—Inouye sending several air strikes against Port Moresby to soften the Australians up for the landing, and Takagi searching in the area near the Solomons, not three hundred miles out.

The Port Moresby invasion force was at sea, twenty-eight ships, carrying a major general and the special south seas detachment that would take over New Guinea. The convoy moved steady south from Rabaul, guarded in the air principally by the light carrier *Shoho*. Captain Ishonosuke Izawa was alert, and kept an air patrol buzzing about the convoy all day long. Twice during the day the convoy was attacked by American bombers. In each case the combat air patrol drove away the attacker—not following far because the duty was to protect the ships, not seek out battle. Late in the day the whole convoy pulled in to the harbor at Shortland Island to fuel and spend the night in comparative safety.

Admiral Fletcher belonged to the careful school of naval officers who worried constantly about battle readiness, and to them much of the problem, from the days of coal, was fuel. It was essential to be ready with plenty of fuel to fight and so fuelling was always on his mind. On May 5 after making the rendezvous, Fletcher's ships spent most of the rest of the day fueling from oiler *Neosho* in a lazy wallowing sea with white clouds overhead and a cool tropical breeze billowing around the ships.

After fuelling, as night fell, Admiral Fletcher changed course, and headed northwest, estimating that any force preparing to attack Port Moresby would steam down from Rabaul. At this time the Port Moresby Invasion force, under Admiral Kajioka, was steaming toward Fletcher. So was the covering group of cruisers and the light carrier *Shoho*. Admiral Takagi and his heavy fleet carriers had left the Tulagi area as unproductive and headed around the south of the Solomons turning.

So the American and Japanese forces were converging, and it was only a matter of time until planes from one sighted the ships of the other. But in spite of the large number of land-based flying boats and search planes of both sides, neither force found the other on May 6. The Americans had Catalina flying boats working out of Noumea, which was too far north. The Americans and Australians had planes working out of Australia, which was too far south, particularly since communications between MacArthur's command and Fletcher had to go roundabout through Pearl Harbor. Thus, although there were many reports of forces including one of three carriers south of the Solomons, Fletcher could make no sense of them.

As for the Japanese, their plan called for the envelopment of the American carrier force. The pincer would be formed by Admiral Goto's cruisers and *Shoho*, and Admiral Takagi's two big carriers. That plan had not changed. The problem was to find the Americans.

On May 6 at 0800 a Japanese scout seaplane confirmed what the loss of such a plane the day before had indicated: an American force was moving northward from a point about 400 miles south of Tulagi. Admiral Takagi then changed course. Instead of heading northwest, he dropped down south, which meant his ships were moving directly toward the American force. That day the Port Moresby invasion force was very nervous; planes drove off several attacking land-based bombers, and because the planes attacked, the Japanese feared they had been discovered by the American task force. Thus after confirmation of the existence of Fletcher's group, Admiral Inouye ordered the transport train to turn back north and stay out of the way, while the two fighting forces under his command crushed the enemy.

Admiral Goto's force, including carrier *Shoho* and the seaplane carrier *Kamikawa Maru* moved in near Deboyne island in the Louisiades, southwest of New Guinea. They were ready for the battle they were sure was coming.

On the ships of the American task force, the sailors were jubilant and eager for action. Lieutenant Commander James Flatley had shot down that Kawanishi flying boat the day before right over the carrier force and the victory had lightened the hearts of everyone. Of course a Kawanishi was not a Zero, and these pilots for the most part had little knowledge of the superior Japanese fighter except by training instruction. But they were eager to fight, and ready for battle on the night of May 6.

That night the combat crews got maps and briefings on the probable course of the action. They studied them carefully before going to their bunks to get a good night's sleep. Aboard the carriers *Shokaku* and *Zuikaku* the Japanese pilots were equally eager; for six months the Japanese had been waiting for the chance to destroy America's carriers. Here, on the morrow seemed to be the opportunity to begin.

Aboard little *Shoho* with her twenty planes, the pilots were also ready for the coming fight. And up in Bandoeng, the Japanese occupation was proceeding without a catch; so successful was the move into the Dutch territories that here just a few months later newspaper correspondents from Japan were brought in to write about the new developments. Sergeant Kawakami and his friends had their pictures taken with prisoners who were having their hair cut, to show the readers of *Yomiuri Shimbun* the beautiful side of a successful war. Japan's empire and her prospects seemed very serene and powerful.

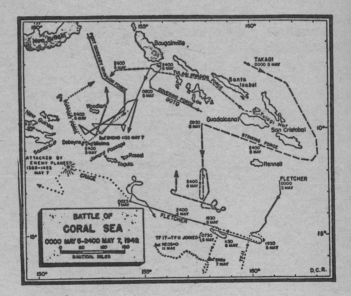

BATTLE OF
CORAL SEA
0000 MAY 5–2400 MAY 7, 1942
0   60   120   180
NAUTICAL MILES

Chapter Six

First Blow

On the evening of May 6, Admiral Fletcher and his staff tried to sort out the various items of intelligence they had been receiving all day long from Pearl Harbor and other sources. They knew that somewhere around them was a large number of Japanese ships, but the reports were conflicting and confusing; virtually everything from submarines to fleet carriers had been reported. Finally Fletcher decided that at least three carriers were in the area and that the Japanese advance was going to come through Jomard passage, up north of them. Admiral Fletcher had hoped to top off his fuel tanks before going into action, but with the seas as they were, it would have meant heading away from the enemy to do so. He had to run north during the night to be in position to launch search planes to confirm all the intelligence reports early in the morning. Radar contacts and one visual sighting of an unidentified plane had suggested that the Japanese knew Fletcher was in the area and more or less what he had to work with. So reluctantly, that evening, Fletcher detached the tanker *Neosho*, giving her destroyer *Sims* as an escort, and sent them off to be out of the way, but available in case of need.

One hour after dawn, *Neosho* and *Sims* were precisely where they were supposed to be—at 16°S, 158°E. At dawn, also Admiral Takagi had a suggestion from Admiral Hara, the carrier division commander. Let Hara send *Zuikaku*'s planes out to search one area behind the carrier force, and *Shokaku*'s planes to search another—just to make sure that the Americans had not circled around and come up in the rear of the Japanese covering force. Takagi approved. The Zeros and the medium bombers revved up and took off from the Japanese carriers, circled and set out at 0600.

At 0736 the Japanese searchers in the eastern section of the zone spotted ships on the water. The observers radioed back to the carriers that they had come upon the American carrier force. Below, said the Japanese observer, were a carrier and a cruiser.

Admiral Hara directed the bombers to the location and the Japanese began to close in. But the ships on which they were moving were not the American carriers, but destroyer *Sims* and oiler *Neosho*.

Just after eight o'clock that morning, lookouts on the *Neosho* spotted two planes, but assumed they were American planes checking on the safety of the oiler and her escort.

Shortly after nine o'clock in the morning Chief Petty Officer Robert James Dicken of the USS *Sims* was sitting in the chiefs' quarters, when he heard a loud explosion. From *Neosho*'s bridge, Captain John S. Phillips could see that a single plane moving over *Sims* dropped that bomb, which exploded about a hundred yards off the starboard quarter of the destroyer.

From the bridge of the *Sims*, Lieutenant Commander Willford Milton Hyman, the captain of the little one-pipe destroyer, passed the order: General Quarters. The ship was under attack. At the moment, some aboard the destroyer thought it was all a dreadful mistake, that one of their own planes had failed to

44

identify the ship and bombed them by mistake. Frantically, the Chief Signalman on the bridge began blinking his light, sending recognition signals. There was no response. The single medium bomber disappeared off to the north.

Captain Hyman ordered full speed. The ship's guns opened up on the retreating bomber, but the plane quickly disappeared into the clouds. *Neosho* changed course to starboard, and *Sims*, the little bulldog, kept out ahead of her, *Neosho* travelling at 18 knots, and *Sims* racing back and forth in front, from port to starboard, the sea swirling in her excited wake.

Fifteen minutes went by, and then twenty. The ships moved on, the lookouts craning around the horizon, squinting into the sun and waiting, sure now that it was no mistake and that there would be more bombs to come. On the bridge Captain Hyman's orders were quiet and terse; it was an eerie time, the whine of the engines driving the propellers, the swish of the sea alongisde the ship, the clang of metal on metal—and still it seemed very, very quiet. Sun and sky and sea had never been more peaceful.

Then, about half an hour after the first attack, little specks, ten of them, appeared in the sky in the north, before the noises of their engines could be heard. The lookouts on *Sims* saw them coming. Captain Hyman called up Captain Phillips to warn *Neosho*; the lookouts of the oiler had not seen the planes. The ships changed course, swung around in a wide arc to throw off the approaching enemy, for now every man on the destroyer and the oiler knew what they must face.

The Japanese pilots saw, and with no effort at all, it seemed, adjusted and came moving in. Still they were very high, paralleling the course of the American ships on their port side. The bombers were so high that although *Sims* began firing rapidly, they were hopelessly out of range.

Sims was an efficient little ship, and her captain had high marks in the service for his gunnery in particular. It was his specialty, dating back to his boyhood when he became an expert rifle shot. In three months time, Captain Hyman would be forty-one years old. More than half that life had been spent in the service of his country, and nearly all the time he had been among the leaders of the battle-ready. He had served for a long time aboard the USS *New Mexico* and had been instrumental in that ship's proud victory over USS *Maryland* for the fleet's Battle Efficiency pennant in 1930. Now, in the face of the enemy, such commendations seemed small turkey indeed, but in the peacetime navy in which he had grown up, such matters had been the making of a career, and Lieutenant Commander Hyman had gone on with a reputation as a potential fighter of the first rank. Service with the staff in Washington had come and gone, then two years at the Naval Powder Factory, followed by two big jobs as a gunnery officer of cruisers, the *Minneapolis* and the *San Francisco,* and the *Quincy.* Seven months earlier he finally got his own ship, the *Sims.*

The Japanese planes were dropping down as they moved away from the ships, and circled to come back at bombing level. Meanwhile other bombers came up, and the Japanese flight leader split the attack in two. Ten planes dove down to make horizontal runs over *Sims,* while another handful moved in on *Neosho,* which was about a mile astern of the destroyer.

To get the range and to give his gunners a feel for their job, Captain Hyman had loaded his ammunition supply so that every tenth shell was starshell. The gunners were trying to draw a bead on the approaching aircraft. From the *Sims* it seemed very satisfactory. Chief Petty Officer Dicken saw from the bridge that the Japanese were staying high and giving the ship's guns plenty of care. All the bombs missed by a wide margin.

Neosho was also under attack. Her captain kept changing course to confuse the planes, and her guns fired as seven bombers came in. The tension grew on the bridge, as the war diary shows:

1006	Changed course to 237°T. Planes paralleled course at high altitude on port side, out of gun range and crossed bow to northeastward; SIMS firing. No bursts were observed. Observed what were believed to be white flares dropped by planes. (These were *Sims*'s star-shells)
1017	Changed course to 187°T.
1023	Sighted approximately seven enemy planes bearing 010°T. *Sims* commenced firing.
1024	Changed course to 242°T.
1025	Changed course to 207°T; commenced firing with 3″/50 caliber guns. Again observed what were assumed to be white flares from planes.
1033	Changed course to 243°T.
1034	Group of 10 planes approached from 140°T, of which three planes (twin-engined bombers) broke off and commenced horizontal bombing attack, others proceeded to northeastward.

Captain Phillips watched the planes as they came in on the oiler; waiting, waiting until he saw the bombs begin to fall. Only then did he move, and ordered the ship put hard aport.

Down came the screaming missiles into the sea, sending geysers of water splashing the air. One bomb hit a hundred yards off the starboard beam, two more were much closer, only 25 yards off target. Had the captain not taken evasive action, they almost certainly would have smashed *Neosho*.

When the attack began, Lieutenant Commander F.J. Firth, the executive officer of *Neosho*, was in the messhall. He was checking on the Abandon-Ship and General-Quarters stations of several seamen from the *Yorktown* and the cruiser *Portland* who had come aboard the ship during the refuelling period, and had been stuck there when *Neosho* was ordered away from the main force during the excitement of the night of May 6.

Commander Firth ran to his action station forward of No. 4 gun on the port side of the stack deck. From that vantage point he watched the attack progress as he waited for reports of damage. When the three bombs fell so close, it was a bad moment. A quick check revealed that there had been no casualties, and no material damage except in the engine room, where those near misses had jarred loose some electrical fittings.

Three minutes after the Japanese planes moved away Captain Phillips changed course again, and ordered the steam smothering system turned on, just in case of fire from a bomb hit.

Sims meanwhile, had beaten off an attack. Captain Hyman turned hard right just as ten bombers dropped their explosives. Only one bomb came anywhere near; the *Sims* moved so quickly, and that one sent a piece of shrapnel slashing through the shoulder of one man on the ship's number 2 gun. Luckily the metal missed bone and arteries, and after the attack the pharmacist's mate bound him up and in a few minutes he was back at his post.

Sims did have one casualty early in the battle, and it shortened her defenses; one of the 20 mm guns jammed, which cut down the 20s by a quarter.

The Number One gun of the main battery was also having problems; after this first set of attacks Captain Hyman noticed that the paint on the gun was blistered from the heat, which meant that all was not well in the barrel.

For nearly an hour and a half, then, the quiet of the sea returned. From time to time, *Sims*'s radarman reported blips on the screen. The Japanese were moving around them, but not a single plane appeared within the glasses of Captain Hyman or Captain Phillips. They watched, and they waited for a renewed attack that must certainly come.

Aboad *Neosho* Captain Phillips instructed his communications officer, a young naval reserve Lieutenant to send out contact reports, first getting the positions right by asking the ship's navigator. But the young officer was badly rattled and failed to do his job properly. Admiral Fletcher would have given a good deal at this moment to know that the planes attacking *Sims* and *Neosho* were carrier planes—he had no idea of the presence of the two big Japanese fleet carriers to the north of him. Actually, at one point during the night, Admiral Takagi had been less than seventy miles away from Task Force 17, but neither commander knew it. As of this morning, they had managed so far to miss one another completely. The young radio officer bollixed up his reports, left most of the detail to an overworked radioman, and the vital word did not get through. Admiral Fletcher, who had been seeing evidences of Japanese land-based air power for days, was not warned.

As the radar contacts came in aboard *Sims*, destroyer and oiler kept changing course, hoping to thwart the enemy. But Admiral Hara was not to be denied. The reports coming back from his carrier pilots only renewed his intention to sink those two American ships, and

49

any others they might find in the vicinity. He sent out a much larger force, and around noon some three dozen Japanese bombers were approaching the two ships.

At 1155, the Chief Signalman was on the bridge when some of those bombers came in sight. As was standard procedure he began blinking, to try to secure recognition. But he knew, and so did everyone else on the bridge, that there would be no response. The silhouettes were familiar now; these were not friendly planes, but the enemy in great force.

Sims opened up with her five-inch guns, and the three unjammed 20 mm antiaircraft guns as well. The boom of the five-inch and the staccato barking of the 20 mm's dominated all sounds; only dimly could the roar of the approaching planes be heard. This time the planes were dive-bombers, not horizontal bombers, and that note should certainly have been passed on by *Neosho*, whose captain was senior officer of the unit. But again, the communications officer failed, and Fletcher did not get the word.

The major attack now was against the "carrier"—*Neosho*—and the Japanese planes came in from astern in three waves. Both ships maneuvered furiously, trying to change the course so quickly and so drastically as to throw off the bombers. Bombs began dropping around *Neosho*, sending up their frightening geysers. They came from bow to quarter, port and starboard, but for a few minutes it seemed the oiler bore a charmed life. Then at 1205 one bomb struck very close by, rattling the plates and knocking out the ship's gyro compass. Captain Phillips ordered the shift to steering by the magnetic compass.

Sims took her first direct hit at 1209. From the bridge of *Neosho* it was a terrible sight, a bomb landed amidships and the section erupted in smoke

50

and flame. Aboard *Sims*, as the smoke cleared, Captain Hyman could see that the bomb had hit near the after torpedo tubes, pierced through the deck, and exploded in the after engine room. The whole deck forward of the after deck house was buckled and torn, tortured black metal sticking crazily up into the air. The number of casualties was not known. The chief engineer, Ensign Tachna, was badly wounded but he stuck to his post, and tried to keep *Sims* going.

In rapid succession two more five-hundred-pound bombs struck *Sims* squarely, and the radar mast fell, dropping squarely across the gig, and immobilizing it. One bomb also smashed the after deck house, and the other struck on Number 4 gun mount, putting that gun out of action.

By this time only two of the ship's five-inch guns were still firing, Number One gun was in bad shape, the heat was so intense at that point that the paint was burning on the gun, and yet the crew stood by and fired it steadily by local control. The fire control system was long gone. Soon the ship began to list heavily, and Captain Hyman summoned Ensign Tachna and the firemen and other engine room personnel out of the wreckage. On deck, Ensign Tachna moved forward, trying to fire the forward torpedo tubes and thus eliminate the danger of an internal explosion. The torpedo deck house was aflame, which meant more danger from the deadly stores within. Tachna led men in putting out that fire, then moved aft for further orders.

In half an hour it was obvious that *Sims* was sinking and that she could not be saved. The job now was to get as many of the men off as possible. Captain Hyman stayed on his bridge, but he ordered all others off. Chief Signalman Dicken went aft to try to flood the after magazines and prevent a dreadful explosion that might cost every life. Dicken could not get aft—the deck between bridge and after deck house was ablaze from starboard rail to port. Ensign Tachna was attempting to put the whale boat into the water. The men from the black gang, more of them uninjured than among the deck crew, came up to help. They took off their shoes and shoved until the boat went over, in spite of the tangled rigging. Two men were aboard, but they were firemen, and not at all skilled in small boat handling. Chief Dicken jumped overboard, swam to the boat, clambered in and took the tiller, then began picking men out of the water as they jumped clear of the foundering destroyer.

At this point the deck between the after deck house and the machine shop was awash, and Captain Hyman ordered Dicken to move back in the whale boat and try to put out that fire in the after deck house. He tried. But he could not get back aboard the Sims—she was already settling aft, and the men in the boat could sense that she was going to go. They pulled clear; just after they got away from the side the boilers blew, and then came a smaller explosion, perhaps a torpedo going off. The ship began to break in two.

Last man off the after section was Machinist's Mate 2c E.F. Munch. Just before he jumped, he stopped and secured a depth charge to the deck so it would not go over the side and kill any men who might be swimming.

Almost immediately the two parts of the Sims separated. The captain was still standing on his bridge in the last moment as the explosion destroyed that section of the ship and both halves sank.

Chief Dicken found himself senior officer of those in Sims's whaleboat, and he directed rescue operations for the next hour and a half. Two life rafts had been shoved over the side in the last few minutes of the destroyer's existence. As soon as the men in the water who were still alive were picked up, he began searching for them. Others in the boat told him they thought there were perhaps twenty other survivors on the life rafts. But Dicken could not find the rafts; they had drifted away somewhere. Counting noses, including his own, he found that he had fifteen survivors, two of them badly wounded. He began pulling for the *Neosho.*

The big oiler, known familiarly to her friends in the fleet as "The Fat Lady," was having her own troubles, and they were nearly as desperate as those of *Sims.*

The real trouble began when the gunners of *Sims* or *Neosho* brought down one of the Japanese dive bombers in flames. Determined not to let the "carrier" escape, and true to the spirit of Bushido, the pilot dove his plane for the deck, and it crashed in the No. 4 gun enclosure, starting a flash fire that spread across the starboard side, aft, knocking out five life rafts. No men of the gun crew were killed, for they had machine guns. But Lieutenant Commander Firth, the ship's executive officer, was at his action station on the port side, just forward of the gun mount, and the explosion knocked him unconscious. The fire got to him before he regained his wits. Badly burned, particularly about the face and arms, he stumbled away from the wreckage, and immediately dispatched a messenger to the bridge to ascertain the captain's orders.

By the time the messenger arrived on the bridge, *Neosho* had taken seven direct bomb hits. The first bomb smashed into the port side of the main deck, tearing a hole fifteen feet along in the port side of the ship. The second bomb penetrated the stack deck, starboard, plunged down into the after center bunker tank, smashing through the ship's store on the way down. It blew the pump room apart, blew an oil tank that let go and caused oil to run all over the forward part of the engine room, and flooded it with six feet of fuel oil. Then the oil caught fire.

The third bomb exploded in the fireroom, killing every man there, knocked out the steam system and the ship's electric power. The fourth blew another huge hole in the ship's port side and caused the main deck to buckle badly. The fifth and sixth bombs blew huge holes in the ship's oil tanks, and so did the seventh, and a near miss—one of eight—did almost as much damage. The other seven bombs were armor piercing, but the near miss was a fragmentation bomb and shrapnel smashed across the bridge, decapitated a machine gunner, killed the rangefinder on the flying bridge, and knocked out the starboard searchlight.

So when Lieutenant Commander Firth's messenger arrived, on the bridge, Captain Phillips knew his ship was in anguish, and wondered how long she might survive. His gunners had stood fast. They had shot down three planes, and thought they had destroyed a fourth, although no one had seen it fall, and three more were seen to falter badly as they swept away after attacking.

But the condition of the oiler was so grave, power out, listing badly, taking water, and with fires burning in several places, that Captain Phillips sent back the word to Lieutenant Commander Firth:

"Make preparations for abandoning ship and stand by."

The messenger retreated aft, where the message was duly delivered. But by this time, the men had seen *Sims* blow up, and some of those aft panicked, Seaman W.D. Boynton, the messenger, reported quite correctly to the executive officer, who was supporting himself unsteadily on the superstructure deck, while several men stood around. Firth gave the orders, and then he collapsed from pain and the shock of his burns. Boynton then repeated the orders, but the men were not listening. Some jumped over the side and began floundering in the water.

On the bridge, Captain Phillips was getting ready for the terrible moment when he would have to abandon his sinking command. He called the communications officer to him, and ordered him to destroy all classified materials—which included the ship's code books. Seeing this, men on the bridge began to panic, and deserted the bridge, shouting that it was every man for himself. The officer of the deck, who was also the navigation officer, was among those panicked, he left the bridge after he heard the captain give the order to flood the ship's magazines. Forward, men were throwing the life rafts overboard, and leaping after them. The navigation officer warned them that they ran the danger of losing the rafts, Other men were trying to launch the Number 1 whale boat, and he ordered a life raft moved so it could be swung out. Thinking twice about his actions, he then headed back for the bridge, but as he moved up, he heard more men coming down, crying "every man for himself" and rushing to throw themselves into the water. The navigator then leaped into the water, along with the enlisted men, as the radio officer and several others tried desperately to launch another boat.

Seeing officers abandoning ship, the men lost all discipline. In a few minutes the water and the rafts were filled with escaping seamen, who were certain the *Neosho*'s end had come.

On the bridge, Captain Phillips watched as so many of his men panicked. He saw that unless he did something, they would drown or be lost on the rafts.

Lieutenant Commander Thomas M. Brown, the gunnery officer, had come down to the bridge to help, after seeing all his people clear of the control tower and the flying bridge from which he had been directing the fire against the Japanese planes. The Japanese were long gone now. Brown addressed himself to the problems of the ship. He helped destroy classified material, called back men who were moving toward the boats, and got the two motor whale boats over the side. The executive officer was unconscious aft, and Lieutenant Commander Brown took over his duties.

Below, Lieutenant Louis Verbrugge, the engineering officer, stayed in the main engine room, until the fire from the bunker tank drove him out. All power was lost. He could sense from the heavy list that there was definite danger the ship might capsize at any moment but he stayed below assessing the damage, and then he went on deck, to report to the captain and supervise the launching of the port motor launch from its skids. With all power gone it was a dreadful job; the starboard boats could not be launched at all, because the seas were breaking over that side of the ship, so deep was her list.

Slowly, through the efforts of the captain, the gunnery officer, and the chief engineer, it became apparent that conditions were not quite as desperate as they had appeared. But most of the men were out of control.

The bomb explosion in the fireroom had terrified many of the survivors. Machinist's Mate First Class Harold Bratt was in charge of the battle station in the after engine room. That compartment was located underneath the fireroom, which was full of live steam, and Bratt advised the four men with him that there was no chance of escaping at the moment, since the only hatch led into the fireroom. But two of the men panicked, they knocked him down and into the bilges, snatched the emergency hand lantern and gas mask he was carrying, and ran up into the fireroom. Bratt and the two others were left below, in darkness, with the compartment slowly filling with cold sea water.

For three-quarters of an hour, Bratt waited there in the gloom, not knowing whether or not the ship would sink beneath him. Finally, feeling that enough steam had escaped from the fireroom above to make their chances almost even, he told his two men to put on gas masks and wrap rags around their arms and hands. When they had done so, he led them up the after escape hatch, and into the fireroom. There they passed the bodies of the two men who had overpowered Bratt and disregarded his orders, and then moved on up to the main deck and comparative safety.

For every coward there were twenty heroes this day. Even among those who panicked, the main reason seemed to be the dreadful shock of seeing *Sims* explode before their eyes.

Machinist's Mate Second Class Wayne Simmons was in the engineroom when one bomb exploded nearby, covering the others with oil from head to toe, and blinding them so they could not see. He helped them out of the engineroom, then manned valves that kept the ship going during the dreadful moments before all power was cut off.

Chief Watertender Oscar Vernon Peterson was standing behind the watertight door that led from the fireroom to the mess compartment, when an explosion blew the door open and knocked him down. Most of Peterson's repair party was killed, and the others were so seriously insured they were out of action. He crawled into the fireroom in spite of his own burns and gashes, and turned off the steam valves—but was terribly scalded in the process, before he could escape the room.

On deck, Chief Pharmacist's Mate Robert W. Hoag and Pharmacist's Mate First Class William J. Ward went to search for the ship's medical officer, but he had been killed by one of the bomb blasts, and they did not even find his body. They set to work, then, to succor the wounded.

But on deck the confusion persisted. The assistant gunnery officer had failed to pass the word when the captain ordered the men to prepare to abandon ship but stand by. And he failed to stop the men from throwing over life rafts and jumping into the water after them. Instead, he went to the Number 2 motor whale boat and began lowering it into the water. He was stopped by Lieutenant Brown, who ordered him to take the boat out, pick up all life rafts and tow them back to the ship, and pick up survivors before they drowned.

The sea was running briskly, four-and five-foot waves slapping up against the sides of the *Neosho*, and some men were thrown against the side of the ship with enough force to injure or knock them out. Others were pulled away by wind and current and still others drowned as the spume and froth of waves choked them and the caps swept down over their heads. Captain Phillips watched in dismay as the assistant gunnery officer made only token efforts to save the struggling men in the water, and did not bring back a single life raft.

Those rafts were scarcely visible from the bridge in the undulating sea for they were dun colored. Against the water even men swimming a few yards from them could not see them over the rising waves. So more men drowned within a few feet of help.

Captain Phillips watched in more dismay as the rafts

began to move out beyond his range of vision. The boats went out, to search, but the seas were not any easier, and they were getting nowhere. The captain could spare only part of his attention to the problem. His main task was to try to restore order to his ship as long as she was afloat.

When the bombs began to fall, nearly all the men of *Neosho* were concentrated in the after section and the bridge. Two gun crews were forward and ammunition and repair parties were stationed near them, but the rest of the ship's company was aft, and the bombs struck aft and in the bridge area. All seven rafts still inflatable had been set afloat, and no one knew how many men had leaped after them. The captain had to find out, and save every man possible. That was the matter at hand.

Chapter Seven

The Death of *Shoho*

The men of Task Force 17 were ready and eager for battle on the morning of May 7, although many of them were dog-tired from long weeks at sea. *Yorktown*, in particular, had been in these southern waters for many weeks, and shortly before this current foray some of the ships had clocked 63 days continually at sea. The men of destroyer *Walke* spoke half in complaint, half proudly of those long days, and how just before pulling into Noumea for resupply their ship had been down to a diet of beans and spaghetti.

From Admiral King's point of view in Washington, the war in the South Pacific was a matter of getting there and stopping the Japanese. From Admiral Nimitz's point of view at Pearl Harbor, it was a matter of doing what he could with the slender resources of his command. From Admiral Fletcher's point of view on *Yorktown* it was a question of moving around stealthily, finding the enemy, and surprising him. From the point of view of the men on the ships it was a matter of scrounging, keeping those ships going, and when the fight came, to do the job. *Walke*, for example, had pulled into Noumea just a few days before this operation, put in at dusk, oiled the ship, carried supplies all night long, and sailed out at daybreak next morning. *Yorktown* had not even put in to port, the hurry was so great.

Now, on the morning of May 7, fatigue was suppressed by surging adrenalin, as the moment of battle came near.

Before dawn, Admiral Fletcher's intelligence indicated that the Port Moresby invasion force, with its transports of soldiers and supplies, was heading toward Jomard Passage from the Rabaul area. This meant the ships would try to slip through between the islands, and then move around northwest, to hit Port Moresby. Even though Admiral Fletcher must concern himself with the fighting ships he knew to be at sea, he could not let the invaders get through. At dawn he dispatched Rear Admiral Crace and his Australian-American force to head the Japanese off at the pass.

His Majesty's Admiral Crace was a good sailor, and he did not question the orders, but set out to do the task assigned him. HMAS *Australia* was in the van, leading the little force: HMAS *Hobart*, USS *Chicago*, and the U.S. destroyers *Farragut*, *Perkins*, and *Walke*. But as Chief Fire Controlman R.F. Spearman of *Walke* put it, "that kind of left us without any aircraft coverage." Every man jack knew that the Japanese carriers were in the area, to say nothing of Japanese land-based air, which had been plastering Port Moresby regularly these last few weeks, and could be expected to go after anything in the waters around that place.

But in fact, *Walke* was a very lucky ship, because she had been scheduled to escort *Neosho* that day until the plan was changed and *Sims* was substituted as the oiler's protector.

The task of Admiral Crace and his force was to move in between Port Moresby and China Strait and wait for the Japanese to come along. Strategists might question the wisdom of Fletcher's separating his force, and sending cruisers and destroyers into Japanese-infested waters without air cover. They moved ahead in a diamond shaped formation, to do the job assigned them. All was serene for about two hours, but then one of those twin-float Japanese spotter planes caught up with the force and began tailing them, staying just out of range of the guns. It was maddening to move on, knowing that up there a radio operator was telling some Japanese admiral precisely who they were and where they were heading, hour after hour.

Having sent off a force to stop the invasion, no matter what happened in the carrier fight he expected, Admiral Fletcher then turned northward. It was quite possible, intelligence told him, that he was facing three carriers somewhere out there.

At this stage of the Pacific war, neither the Japanese nor the American pilots were very expert in the identification of aircraft. They were less so in the identification of ships. Of course for the most part when pilots came across unknown ships they were flying at high altitude, and they were often hampered by cloud cover. Their observations consisted of quick glimpses of vessels below, from which they must make a judgment and deliver a report. That was why the pilots of *Yorktown* made such an inaccurate appraisal of their victory at Tulagi, and why the Japanese fliers from Admiral Hara's carrier force thought they were hitting a carrier and a cruiser, instead of oiler *Neosho* and her little escort *Sims*.

Now, on the morning of May 7, as the Japanese found *Neosho* and thought she was a carrier, *Yorktown*'s planes were making as significant an error. *Yorktown* launched ten dive bombers just before seven o'clock in the morning, with directions to conduct a single plane search. The compass was divided up like a pie, with one plane responsible for a certain sector or wedge of it. Not quite two hours after launch, one of the scouts reported back that he had found two carriers and four heavy cruisers about 175 miles away on the northeast side of the Louisiade island group. The report was later discovered to be inaccurate, the result of a mechanical error. The pilot had a contact pad at hand, in a special holder, and the pad was improperly lined up. The pilot saw a destroyer and check, but where he made the mark indicated a cruiser. So the mistake was made. Another scout found two cruisers not far away, they challenged the plane with searchlight flashes, but of course the American could not reply. Other scouts shot down two Kawanishi flying boats. The scouts in the sector with median 067° went out 165 miles, and then turned back, foiled by heavy weather. Thus *Yorktown's* search missed Admiral Takagi's fleet carriers altogether.

The erroneous report sent excitement through the U.S. task force, and the air officers of the carriers bent to action. What the scout had actually sighted was Admiral Marumo's force, two old light cruisers, a seaplane carrier, and three converted gunboats. But no one aboard *Yorktown* or *Lexington* knew that.

Lexington was ready to launch first, for she had not had the responsibility of the search that morning. The weather was very spotty as Captain Frederick Sherman turned her into the wind. Visibility was at most ten miles, and that was cut to three-quarters of a mile when the ship ran into a rain squall, but there were enough breaks to launch planes. At 0925 *Lexington's* attack group began swooping off the carrier. The pilots brought their planes to the launch line, increased the power until the planes shuddered in vibration, then released the brakes, rushed down the long narrow deck to the end, and either lifted just as the carrier's bow rose, or dropped slightly off the edge before recovering and climbing. In a few minutes ten fighters, 28 dive bombers and a dozen torpedo bombers were in the air, headed for the enemy position near the Louisiades. Admiral Fitch was committing his force; only eight dive bombers were retained on the carrier for anti-torpedo plane patrol.

Only after the force was committed did the word come that the *Yorktown* search pilot had made an error. Captain Sherman believed this meant there were no carriers when they had been reported, but Admiral Fitch allowed the mission to continue. There was something out there, and to bring the planes back would be wasteful and might accomplish absolutely nothing.

The Japanese were in action, too. Since the day before, Japanese observation planes had been shadowing the American Task Force and reporting on activity. Admiral Goto, director of the Port Moresby invasion forces, was ready for an attack, and the light carrier *Shoho*, the basic protective arm, was ready, too. But back at Rabaul, Admiral Inouye did not want to risk the transports until the outcome of the approaching air battle between big carriers was decided, so the transports, which were lurking off the Louisiades, waiting to make the turn through Jomard passage, were still held back, pending the destruction of the American threat.

At 0515 *Shoho* was rigged for battle and fifteen minutes later four fighters and an attack bomber were launched to cover the transports.

At 0630 Admiral Goto's flagship, the cruiser *Aoba*, reported that the American task force was 140 miles away and 160° off Deboyne island. Knowing that much, Captain Izawa made preparations to launch a strike against the Americans. All the 80 officers and 700 men were eager for battle. The four fighters and attack bombers were called back from the convoy, since it was pulling out of danger and could be covered by land-based air. They landed on the carrier to refuel and reload just after three fighters took off to form the combat air patrol and ward off enemy attack.

Commander W.B. Ault was leading the strike from *Lexington* and after he passed Tagula island in the Louisiades he began looking for the force described by the *Yorktown* from its morning search. Lieutenant Commander W.L. Hamilton looked down through the clouds and spotted a carrier, at least two cruisers, and several destroyers off to starboard. This was *Shoho* and her support ships.

The group turned. Commander Ault led his two wingmates in the dive on the carrier. Two of the Zeros zoomed up to 15,000 feet, to attack the Americans, just as Captain Izawa spotted the American force and saw it split to begin the bomb runs. Izawa then began a violent zigzagging, turning and pirouetting, making the sea boil in curlecue pattern behind the carrier, as she dodged and switched to throw the bombers off. Ault and his wingmates bored in, and the fighters—those incredible swift, slippery Zeros— were after them in a moment. One Zero slashed in to hit the bomber of Lieutenant Allen, executive officer of the scouting squadron, and shot him down, as the bombers ran in from astern. The other two planes began diving from a point a thousand yards off the stern, nosed over steeply, and pulled out of three thousand feet. It was not close enough—the bombs missed, but one of them was close enough to blow five planes off the deck of *Shoho*.

The other *Lexington* planes now spread out to attack from the starboard side, as Captain Izawa pushed the ship into the wind, so he could launch another three fighters.

On his approach, Lieutenant (jg) Quigley felt his dive bomber hit by anti-aircraft fire from the carrier, and the plane became sluggish. A shell had shot away the control wires. He reported to Ault, who ordered him to make for Rossel Island in the Louisiades. No Japanese had been reported on the island and it was still considered friendly allied territory. Ault got back to fighter control aboard the ship. He reported the event, in the hope that *Lexington* would notify air headquarters at Townsville so the Americans or Australians could arrange for Quigley's rescue if he made it down safely or bailed out over the island. Then *Lexington's* planes, fighters, dive bombers, and torpedo planes, became part of a milling, screaming attack that was quickly joined by planes from *Yorktown*, until there were ninety-three planes in all involved in the attack, against the nine fighters Captain Izawa was able to throw into the air.

Aboard *Yorktown*, Captain Elliott Buckmaster had also launched his attack group on receipt of the faulty report from his scout. Eight fighters, seven dive bombers, seventeen scout bombers and ten torpedo planes joined the *Lexington* group over *Shoho* shortly after the attack began, and they were much more heavily armed than *Lexington's* bombers. Ault's planes were carrying one five-hundred-pound bomb and two one-hundred-pound bombs, but the *Yorktown* planes were loaded with 100-pound Mark 13 bombs. Torpedo planes from both carriers were armed with Mark 13 torpedoes, and those of *Yorktown* were set for a depth of ten feet, to pass below the armor belt of a carrier.

Officers and men of both U.S. carriers listened to the progress of the attack, as it was reported by the pilots. They were eager to hear how the Japanese reacted, for this was the first big ship-to-ship battle in which the Americans had faced the enemy.

The pilots kept up a running commentary as they zeroed in on the carrier. They noted that the Japanese ships had scattered instead of forming a ring around *Shoho*, which would have magnified their anti-aircraft strength. Yet, it was remarkable to the pilots, how quickly and deftly the Japanese ships maneuvered at high speed.

Captain Izawa, having avoided the first *Lexington* attack, had made a tactical error in turning into the wind to launch, for it held his ship steady, and just then, as the planes cleared the decks, *Lexington*'s second wave and *Yorktown*'s bombers arrived. The Japanese fighters were not even in position to slow them down as they plunged in.

As Captain Izawa completed the launch, he discovered the error, two torpedo wakes appeared off to starboard, and immediately he ordered the helm pushed hard to starboard to head past them, and the torpedoes missed.

But three minutes later, the bombers were on him, and two bombs struck the forward part of the rear elevator on the flight deck, smashing it inward and then up, so that the metal hung high above the deck, a crazy corner bent over and pointing out to sea. Below, the bombs set fire on the hangar deck where the planes and their gasoline supply were stored, and began inching toward the torpedo room.

Captain Izawa ordered the damage control parties to work, but even as he did so, several torpedoes struck the stern on the starboard side, and almost immediately the explosions knocked out the ship's electric power system, and blasted the steering to bits. Then came more bombs, more torpedoes, and even manual steering was destroyed—the ship's rudder was gone.

Up above, the Japanese fighters gave their all—but how much could they accomplish when the odds were greater than ten to one? The American pilots, meeting the Zero and its float-plane counterpart for the first time, were surprised at the ability of the pilots. (According to American mores, Japanese all wore bottle-bottom glasses, had buck teeth, hissed "Ah, sso." constantly, and faked American manufactures). The fliers of *Lexington* and *Yorktown* discovered strange defensive devices unknown previously (and afterwards): the Japanese planes apparently were all equipped with smoke-making devices, so they emitted smoke when in a tight spot, caused their attackers to drop away and then zoomed off to fight again. The Japanese planes also carried special flares or grenades delivered from the rear of the plane. But one truth they did discover this day: the Imperial General Staff had made one miscalculation that would cost them dearly before the war ended: the Zero's maneuverability was partly occasioned by its light weight; but the Zero pilot had no armored seat or even a self-sealing fuel tank, and so one well-placed burst of machine gun fire could kill the pilot or flame the plane. It was the most important discovery of the day.

As for their own planes, the Americans made another discovery rather proof of something some pilots had been claiming for a long, long time. The TBD torpedo bomber was totally unsatisfactory. It was too slow, which meant the dive bombers were always miles ahead and sometimes many minutes. This meant that when the dive-bombers arrived at the target they had to mill around, waiting for the torpedo planes, which warned the enemy, or go in alone, which blunted the full force of the high-lo attack. Casualties were going to be high unless all carriers could soon have the new TBFs, said the *Yorktown*'s air group leader. How right he was would be shown just a month later in the battle of Midway when Commander John C. Waldron's whole Torpedo 8 squadron, flying the old TBDs, would be slaughtered in attacking the Japanese carriers.

Lieutenant Commander Brett of *Lexington*'s VT-2 led that ship's group in, and the pilots claimed nine hits on this carrier, which at the moment was misidentified as the *Ryukaku*. The mistake was forgivable, *Shoho* had originally been the transport *Tsurugasaki*, and she had been converted in 1941 to a light carrier, but the christening had not been held until after the Pearl Harbor attack was launched; Jayne's fighting ships did not have her, and the American naval attachés who might have identified the ship were no longer moving around Japan.

Now, *Shoho* was in her death throes. Bombs and torpedoes smashed and shocked her from one end to the other, turning an orderly ship into a mass of smoking wreckage. The communications system failed, the power shot out. The engines stopped, when torpedoes smashed into the boiler rooms, and she began to slow to a stop. Well-placed bombs knocked out the main anti-aircraft guns, and their twisted barrels looked down on the blood flowing on the deck where once stood a living gun crew. The dead lay on the decks, unattended, sprawled on the ladders, leering in the companionways. The wounded piled against the bulkheads, seeking the dubious shelter of metal walls against the explosives cascading down from the sky.

The groans of the wounded and the cries of the men still fighting mingled in the deafening background. The handful of guns still firing were running on manual control; the gunners had no shortage of targets, there were so many, moving so fast, that it was like trying to swat at a swarm of Canadian blackflies.

Ten minutes after the attack began, the ship was in flames. Above, the attackers were trying to take photographs, and when they were developed, they showed only the bow of *Shoho*—the rest of the ship was totally enveloped in smoke and flames.

The Japanese damage-control parties faced a hopeless task. They tried to fight the fires, but the water pressure slowed and died, leaving men holding empty, limp hoses, with the flames crackling ahead of them. Below, others tried to shore up the holes in the ship made by torpedoes and bombs, some twenty torpedoes, some fifty bombs, and of course they could not. Men drowned and died bravely, but the water kept rushing in.

By 0920 (Japanese time estimate), thirty minutes after the first dark spots had been seen in the sky over *Shoho*, she was sinking, and water had risen to the gun deck. Still she fought, although dead in the water, and around her the support ships kept hurling up their anti-aircraft fire as well; in the air, the Japanese fighters zoomed and squirreled, going after the planes that were killing their ship.

Yorktown's dive bombers came in steeply over the bow of the carrier from 18,000 feet, dropped at 2,500 feet, and pulled out. The destruction was so certain that the last bomber pilot, seeing what his companions had done, turned and sought another target; he picked a ship he described as a cruiser, bombed her, and watched her sink. Several other pilots confirmed the sinking and so did the Staff Gunnery Officer, although no Japanese cruiser was lost that day. But from 18,000 feet, a patrol boat might look like a cruiser through a haze of smoke and cloud, to an excited pilot on his first combat mission. Some small craft were lost in the Coral Sea action, so insignificant as not to ever have been counted in the allied totting up at the end of the war.

Last, *Yorktown's* torpedo planes made their run from the starboard side of the carrier. As they came in they saw her heavy list, and devastating fires. At least they saw fires everywhere, and only the bow of the ship. By this time only two small AA guns were still firing, with little effect, The torpedo pilots came in very close, dropped, and claimed ten hits out of ten drops.

Three minutes after those torpedoes struck home, it was all coming to an end. Captain Izawa ordered his crew to abandon ship, and the sailors who could still move began dropping over the side, while the support ships circled, prepared to rescue the survivors. Four more minutes, and the ship plunged to the bottom, carrying down six hundred and thirty-one members of the crew. Seventy-two more, wounded, were able to get off and maintain themselves in the water until help arrived. But of the proud crew that had begun fighting that day, only a hundred and thirty-two were in condition to fight again, and *Shoho* had lost many valuable pilots and air crew members.

At the moment of sinking, *Shoho* still had six fighters in the air, and they made good account of themselves. They went after the *Yorktown* group as if they had been sixty, and were joined by at least one land-based plane. The American fighters had been divided into two sections, four planes assigned to protect the dive bombers and four to protect the torpedo planes. The pilots had been warned not to try to "dog-fight" with the more maneuverable Zeros, but to use superior speed and diving ability to strike, then climb and strike again. The Japanese tried to lure them down on the deck, down to fifty feet off the water, pulling into sharp Immelmann turns and loops, and corkscrewing back up to hit the bombers. A Japanese turned onto the tail of one of the torpedo bombers, but was driven off by a slashing fighter attack, and only damaged the plane. They were heading for those bombers, they damaged three of them, but caused no casualties, as the fighters did their protective job. But two of the fighters fell, to the more maneuverable Zeros, and their skilful pilots, and three of the six Japanese fighters were shot down, as well as the land-based scout plane that had come to help them.

At the end, as the Americans began winding home, one dive bomber pilot forgot all he had ever learned about the enemy, and in his verve dropped out of formation to engage in combat with a Zero. It was no contest. In a few minutes the dive bomber began to smoke, and headed down to crash in the sea, a reminder to the pilot's comrades to obey their orders and stick to the job at hand.

Below, the destroyer *Sazanami* was picking up the pitiful remainder of *Shoho*'s crew, as the droning of the American planes drifted into silence above the sea. The three surviving Japanese fighters took one last look around, found the skies empty, and looked at their gas gauges. They headed for Deboyne island, and all were lucky enough to crash land there, saving pilots if not planes to fight another day.

Heading back to their ships, the Americans were jubilant, and there was much laughter on the air waves as the pilots talked to their ships. Then came the statement that was to thrill all America when it was heard, an America hard-pressed by a dismal succession of stories of surrenders in the Philippines, battles lost, and great ships sacrificed; it was the crow of Lieutenant Commander R.E. Dixon, second in command of *Lexington*'s dive bombers.

"Dixon to carrier," he shouted into his microphone, "Scratch one flattop."

And when the grinning aircrews landed on their carriers that day their air of satisfaction over a job well done almost obscured the fact, known very well to Admirals Fletcher and Fitch, that the main battle had not yet even begun.

The pilots of *Lexington* and *Yorktown* wanted to get back again as soon as they could rearm and gas up, and finish the job. There were still those four cruisers and the destroyer out there, and Captain Buckmaster of *Yorktown* and Captain Sherman of *Lexington* had the job in hand, but Admiral Fletcher voted them down. There *was* an enemy carrier force out there, and the Americans had not yet located it, although Fletcher knew the Japanese had located him, and the word of the strike against *Shoho* would put an urgency to Japanese action.

Up above the Louisiades, Admiral Goto moved his cover force, now less *Shoho*, off to the northeast. Only the seaplane carrier *Kamikawa Maru* remained in the Deboyne island area.

Japanese air intelligence reports to Admiral Takagi before and after the sinking of *Shoho* had pretty well established the area in which the American carrier force must be operating. Admiral Takagi decided in mid afternoon to launch a strike that would find the American ships at sundown, the time he estimated they would be least on the lookout and most vulnerable. Fifteen torpedo planes and a dozen bombers took off at 1430 and headed for the area around 150 miles southeast of the Louisiades. The weather here was very squally in the afternoon, with ninety percent overcast, and sudden little cloudbursts which brought visibility down to zero. Consequently, the Japanese missed the carriers entirely, flew past them, hidden in the murk, and searched barrenly in the area beyond. But the planes were spotted on the carriers' radar out west of the task force, and as they headed back for their own carriers, Admiral Fitch's fighter control vectored the combat air patrol out to intercept the Japanese, who were then eighteen miles off, and began to launch more planes, some to guard the ships, some to move out and hit the enemy.

Lieutenant Commander Paul Ramsey led the first group of fighters, and soon the men in the carrier radio room heard him talking to his wingmen. They had found a flight of nine Zeros heading for the carrier at five thousand feet. They attacked, and in the wardroom of *Lexington*, where the radio was constantly tuned to the fight frequencies, the officers of the ship heard a running account of the battle.

The poor weather put a premium on the American tactics of hit and run, rather than stay with the Zeros and slug it out. Flying in and out of cloud, to find the enemy was the problem, but the battle was joined by planes from both carriers, and raged from the attack point at 5000 feet down to just above the water.

The Americans shot down all nine Japanese fighters that day, with a loss of two of their own. One of these, Lieutenant (jg) Paul G. Baker, had just shot down a Zero—his wingman Ensign Edward Sellstrom saw it—when he turned into another Japanese plane, and they collided head on, and both burst into red flaming balls that fell into the sea. The second American fighter's experience brought that poignant, silencing tale that carrier pilots dreaded. Safe in the battle,

74

this pilot became disoriented and lost on the way home in the murk and the gathering night, and his carrier *Yorktown* was far away. Through the fleet, where all available radios were turned to the fighter frequency, the men heard him talking to *Yorktown* and to fighter control, who were trying to talk him in. But an hour went by, and there was no welcome sound of a droning F4F engine. He reported laconically that he was very nearly out of fuel, and must prepare to ditch. Then, with new hope, he said he saw, faintly in the clouds below him, the outline of an island, and he was going to try to land down there. He went down, and that was the last transmission. No one knew what island, or where he had landed. If it was Deboyne, he was in deep trouble, but otherwise he might have a chance, for the natives of the area were generally loyal to the Australians and their allies, and the Japanese would not get him.

As darkness fell, and the crackling of the radio died out, the officers assembled in their messes to dine. In the Junior Officers' mess, where most of the pilots ate, the place was a bedlam as the young men reenacted their experiences of the day. On *Lexington* they were telling their tales excitedly to one another and the ship's complement of officers, when suddenly, a tremendous racket broke loose above. Somewhere AA guns began firing and men were running across the flight deck.

On came the emergency circuit of Talk-Between-Ships, and *Yorktown* spoke up.

"Lex, how many planes do you have in the air?"

"We've only got four, how many have you got?"

"We've only got two, and there's a hell of a sight more out there than that."

Then a destroyer spoke up. She had recognized one

of those planes as a Japanese torpedo bomber, and had begun firing.

All the ships then opened up, and the fighters above looked around for the Japanese, some of whom had moved into a landing pattern, for they had mistaken the American carriers for their own, and were trying to "come home."

The night was lit up like a Fourth of July fireworks display at Coney Island, in the old days, star shells arcing across the fleet, and tracers burning red and blue as they hissed out through the air. The Japanese turned and sped away to find their own ships, and the American planes were brought in as night closed around the Task Force.

Then, half an hour later, *Lexington*'s radar showed specks orbiting about thirty miles to the east, and when Admiral Fitch was so advised, he deduced that these were Japanese planes in a landing circle around a carrier. He passed the word to Fletcher, the word was delayed, and by the time Fletcher got it he was in no mood to launch a night attack. A night attack by the Americans at that point in the war would have been a very iffy business at best, for American night fighter techniques were very elementary, and Japanese ship handlers were far more adept as the forthcoming night fights at Guadalcanal would show. They should have been, the Japanese had been training for night actions for a dozen years, while the whole concept was just being developed in the American navy.

So under the circumstances, although the Japanese were almost on their doorstep, the Americans backed off and waited for morning before attempting to continue the battle. The Japanese, from their viewpoint, were in no position to launch a night attack just then. The incoming torpedo bombers arrived in total darkness, Admiral Hara, the air commander, had to turn on the ship's searchlights (a very risky business which was to make Admiral Marc Mitscher a national hero when he did it at the first battle of the Philippine Sea two years later.)

Admiral Inouye, the overall commander of the operation, considered a night attack, but changed his mind. At 1700 and thereabouts, American and Japanese admirals could place their respective carriers close together, but four hours later it was quite a different matter. Conceivably they could be two hundred miles apart. Admiral Takagi was ready: a dozen of his planes had been lost in the night landing on the carrier, nine Zeros were missing, and it was time the enemy be brought to account for the sinking of *Shoho*. But Rear Admiral Koso Abe, commander of the Port Moresby transports, asked for the carriers to move in and protect his ships, now that *Shoho* was gone, and Admiral Takagi's mission here was to cover the invasion force, not destroy the American fleet, so Admiral Hara was ordered to head north, not west, while Admiral Fletcher headed southeast to wait for morning.

Chapter Eight

Crace's Chase

His Majesty's Admiral Crace, with whatever misgivings he might have about heading into enemy waters where he knew the Japanese land-based airplanes would be giving heavy cover, took his little combined fleet of Australian and American ships steadily toward the corner of the Louisiades where the Japanese invasion force might be slipping through. The speed was 25 knots.

The speed of travel toward the enemy was not so great, for the diamond formation moved in zigzags to avoid enemy submarines that would have a sitting duck party on any force, no matter how fast it moved, if it travelled in a straight line. The zigzag was American pattern No. three, no trouble for the British for it was their pattern Number 9.

All was well until around 1400. The ships were travelling on a base course of 290°. The wind was at eight knots from the southeast, and the sea was following but a bit choppy, the weather generally fair, with forty percent cumulous clouds at about 6000 feet, a day that in peacetime would have been a bright, beautiful time to be at sea.

For two or three hours, the force had been followed by three twin-engined Japanese bombers, which kept disappearing in the clouds, turning around, going no one knew where, then reappearing. There was obvious method in the Japanese action, one plane trailed the formation, the other two were on the sides of it; all flew at low altitude and all stayed safely out of gun range.

When the Japanese planes first came up, the task group excitedly went to general quarters. But as the hours droned on and nothing happened, Admiral Crace saw that there was no use maintaining tension—trouble would come soon enough—so the ships went to Condition Two. All boilers were kept in readiness for use; the guns were out and ready, the ammunition was ready, and radar conducted a continuous circling search above the ships.

At 1427 lookouts aboard USS *Farragut* spotted ten Japanese planes, apparently chasing an American carrier plane. Lookouts aboard *Chicago* saw a dozen planes, and *Chicago* began firing. The other ships joined in, and soon five-inch guns were sending up a barrage of white puffs.

The enemy planes were low on the water—that is why they were able to come so close without being tracked by radar. They jinked, passed along the port side and ahead of the formation without any attempt to attack, broke their formation, and scudded out of range.

Fifteen minutes later *Chicago*'s radar picked up a group of planes 30 miles away, but closing in from a bearing of 250°. The group changed course, steered 230° for seven minutes and changed course again to 275°, but two minutes later the planes were still closing, now 18 miles away by radar count.

Six minutes passed, and a lookout spotted the planes, flashing in the sun at 25,000 yards. Admiral Crace changed course to 290°, as the planes began their approach, gliding down to 100 feet above the water—horizontal Japanese approach from far out;

torpedo planes bearing their deadly gifts, and heading straight for *Australia*.

One by one the American and Australian ships began firing. Spotters identified the Japanese bombers as Mitsubishi 97s or medium bombers. They were brought in by fighters, but as there was no air interception, the fighters swung on out to look around, while the three groups of four planes each, headed in, bound for the ships.

Destroyer *Farragut* took bead on one of the leading planes at five thousand yards, and made a direct hit. The plane went plummeting into the sea. *Walke* also thought her gunners had hit this plane, or the one immediately behind it, for it too crashed, a flamer.

From his bridge, Admiral Crace watched closely.

Aircraft commenced the approach at about 1000 feet, diving and losing height in a shallow dive to about 100 feet, when they adopted a loose formation. They opened out somewhat on reaching the barrage but no attempt was made to attack simultaneously from both bows of the task group. "Australia's" alteration to port to avoid torpedoes enabled two wing aircraft, however, to work in an attack from her starboard bow. All aircraft dropped torpedoes at ranges between 1,000 and 1,500 yards and the majority of them continued to fly over the ships, "strafing" them with machine and cannon gun.

The men on the ships watched as the planes dropped their fish—some outside the formation, some waiting until they had come inside the perimeter of ships. Admiral Crace counted eight torpedoes, three aimed at *Australia*, four at *Chicago*, and one at *Hobart*.

Commander T.E. Fraser, captain of *Walke*, gave a

very good idea of how it was in his account of the battle:

Fire was continued with full battery as ship was brought to right to unmask entire battery and the second salvo apparently hit the leading plane, causing it to burst into flames and crash just ahead of *Perkins*. The plane next in line either ran into the flaming plane or was hit, and it, too, crashed. Fire was continued until the line of fire was blocked by *Perkins*.

20 mm machine gun fire from No 2 and No 4 machine guns was commenced as planes came within range. While passing down port side smoke and flame was observed coming from two of these planes as they dropped torpedoes at the *Australia* one from a position just off the port quarter of *Perkins*, and the other on the starboard bow of the *Australia*. This second plane banked sharply toward the *Australia* just before launching her torpedo. One plane crashed on the starboard quarter of this vessel, after passing ahead of the *Chicago*. Three planes on the port side of *Australia* were observed to drop torpedoes at the *Chicago*, after which one crashed just off the *Australia's* port quarter. . . .

On *Farragut* they opened up with everything they had, even Thompson sub-machine guns and Browning automatic rifles. The planes were so close, flying in the ship formation, that these small guns might possibly do some good.

In five minutes the attack was ended, but immediately the formation was hit by high flying bombers, estimated in number somewhere between nineteen and twenty-six by various watchers.

For a time sailors on the *Walke* believed the *Australia* must have sunk—she was straddled by so many bombs that the splashes concealed the ship from the others. But the high level bombing was easier to take. The planes maneuvered and fired, and *Farragut* was very lucky. Two big bombers came after her and Comdr. G.P. Hunter, her captain, came hard left as they dropped, increased to flank speed, and the bombs, five of them, missed by two hundred yards, but hit just where *Farragut* would have been had the captain not taken evasive action.

In ten minutes the big high-flying bombers had made their attempt, and they too were driven off without sinking or seriously damaging a ship. The gunners stood at the ready, an hour and a half later a shadow was with them again, a two-pontoon seaplane that followed them about three miles back, telling someone somewhere just what the allied ships were doing. For an hour and fifteen minutes the plane followed them, then as dusk began to fall it turned away to head back to its base. From time to time during the evening more plane reports came in but no further attacks were mounted, and the ships began cleaning up the damage, treating the wounded, and getting the dead ready for burial.

Chicago had seven wounded—two of them so seriously they died: Seaman First Class A.B. Shirley, Jr., and Baker Third Class R.E. Reilly. Shirley had been gun pointer on AA gun No 5, and was hit in the head by a piece of shrapnel. Reilly, a lookout, was also hit in the head.

Five others, Gunner's Mate Third Class W.R. Moore, Seaman First Class H. E. Dettman, Ship's Cook Second Class M.R. Johnson, Gunner's Mate Third Class H.L. Long, and Electrician's Mate Third Class R.W. Greer received less serious wounds, some of them from machine-gun fire from the strafing planes.

On *Farragut*, Seaman First Class H. E. White was grazed by a Japanese machine gun bullet, and got just enough of a laceration over his right eye to win a Purple Heart. He was a very lucky man.

That was the end of the action. At least it was the end of action by the enemy. Almost immediately a group of high-flying B-17s came over, American planes, and bombed *Farragut* from 33,000 feet. Men on the ship saw the planes and their insignias very clearly through their glasses, although General Mac-Arthur's air commander later flatly denied the bombing. It was not unusual—the army men were not at all used to seeing American ships in these waters. For months they had seen nothing but Japanese vessels. It would take them a while to learn to tell friend from foe—and meanwhile the men of *Farragut* cussed out the Air Corps in no uncertain terms.

By midnight, Admiral Crace had reached a position off New Guinea, and he continued to follow the coast for a while, but then the word came that he was wasting his time—the Port Moresby invasion force had turned around and was far away. So Crace headed back toward Australia. *Farragut* lost her starboard engine next day, and had to put into Brisbane for repairs. So the engagement known as Crace's Chase ended. It was of so little importance in the strategical scheme of things that it rated only a few paragraphs in the history books, yet Americans and Japanese died in that brief air battle—five Japanese torpedo bombers were shot down, and American sailors were killed in defending their ships. The war was with them every minute, and in saving their ships and destroying the enemy, the men of Crace's force had done quite a remarkable job.

The Japanese pilots, who were as capable of self-deception as any, came home from that fight with Crace's force to report that they had sunk one battleship and damaged two cruisers. But the fact was they had sunk nothing at all.

Chapter Nine

The Ordeal of *Neosho*

Captain Phillips's basic concern was to get his ship
back under control, for even if she sank, he would
have to try to save the lives of all those he could, and
without the taut discipline of the navy, there was
little chance of saving anything. The chief engineer
made a trip below to see if there was any chance of
raising steam, but the whole power plant of the ship
had been wrecked by the bombs, and there was no
way at all it could be repaired. So the captain had to
resign himself to drifting and waiting for help.

At 1445 the Chief Signalman of the *Sims* appeared alongside *Neosho* in the one living boat of
that ship, and with his fourteen men—all that remained of the whole ship's complement of a
destroyer. He and others believed there were more
survivors on the two rafts they had seen drifting away
from the side of *Sims* before she blew up, but they
had not found them, nor had they seen any sign of
the rafts after Dicken had finished picking survivors
out of the water. Now Dicken placed himself and his
men under the orders of Captain Phillips and asked
what he could do.

Captain Phillips took the *Sims*'s wounded aboard
and turned them over to Pharmacists Hoag and
Ward, who were giving morphine, bandaging
wounds, and swabbing out bloody holes in the flesh

of the survivors and trying to comfort the burned men. The captain then instructed Dicken to circle *Neosho* and pick up any swimmers in the water. *Sims*'s complement joined the *Neosho* survivors at the port rail, where Captain Phillips had kept them for the past hour in anticipation that the ship might founder, and they would have to leap for their lives.

As the sun sank in the sky, *Neosho* continued to settle in the water and her list became more profound. Captain Phillips was very worried. He ordered the radio officer to get the fix from the navigator that had been made during a lull in the fighting, and to send out a call for help. It would have to be in the clear, since he had destroyed the code books. That meant running the danger of being rescued by the Japanese, but the ship was in extremis, and there was no alternative. So the radio officer got the information from the navigator and sent off a message.

The navigator had plotted their position as Latitude 16°, 25′ South and longitude 157°, 31′ East. With that information, even accepting the vagaries that would be caused by their drifting without any power at all, Admiral Fletcher's task force should be able to find them within twenty-four hours. All they had to do was hold on.

Neosho's two whale boats and the *Sims* boat ranged wide out from the ship, searching and picking up men until 1800. As dusk began to fall, they came in, all of them badly overloaded, moving gingerly in the rough sea, until they reached the ship's side. Only then did Captain Phillips learn that *Sims*'s boat had so great a gash in the hull that it kept afloat only because Dicken had stuffed it with a mattress, and his men bailed constantly.

Five of the men of *Neosho* who were in best condition had been ordered into the water off the port side, to keep a minimum of personnel aboard the sinking hulk, and now they were picked up by the *Sims*'s boat. There were so many injured that they could not all be moved back to the shrinking deck of *Neosho* and Captain Phillips ordered the whale boats to fend off, and remain not closer than fifty yards off the port side of the ship during the night.

As darkness fell the able-bodied men of *Neosho* got ready for what might come. They tore all the standing rigging and extra gear out of the two motor launches that were pinioned to the ship by the fall of debris and the lack of power, in the hope that if *Neosho* sank during the night, they would float clear and could be used. They gathered mess tables and benches, and the objects they could find that would float, and brought them to the port side, where they would float clear as the ship sank and give the men some kind of chance, waiting for dawn when Fletcher's rescue party would surely be there at their side.

Lieutenant Verbrugge, the engineer, went below again, to see what he could salvage, but there was very little, and once again he came back to report mournfully that there was no chance of getting up steam.

The captain sent men to repair the transmitting antenna, which was found to be broken, so the messages to the task force would get through. The radio men manned the auxiliary gasoline generator to send the word.

Captain Phillips took a muster of survivors. He found that of 21 officers and 267 men aboard *Neosho* that morning before the attack, there were now 16 officers and 94 men aboard, plus the fifteen survivors of *Sims*. One officer was known to have been killed (the medical officer) and nineteen men were dead; but four officers and one hundred and fifty-four men were missing, the result of the panic and misunderstanding of orders that had sent them scrambling over the side of the ship during the Japanese attack. Captain Phillips was concerned, but he knew that most of these people had made it to the safety of the life rafts, and he was certain that next day the search planes of the two big carriers would locate the men and they would be rescued, perhaps even more quickly than the men of *Neosho* itself.

There was a good deal to be done to save the ship, if such was possible. The captain kept a close watch on the inclinometer, which showed the relative stability of the vessel. The list was 30 degrees. It would have grown worse except that Captain Phillips opened the valves to the starboard wing tanks, which filled them with sea water, and tended to counteract the port weight.

There was one big worry. The main-deck plating was continuing to buckle under the conflicting pressures, and this gave the captain much cause for concern. Lt. Verbrugge reported that the engine room and fireroom were taking more water in the evening than they had been in the daylight hours, and it was quite noticeable.

As darkness fell, the captain issued his orders: there were to be absolutely no lights shown—flashlights or lamps or any others. There was to be quiet, and the men were to get as much rest as they could during the night, while they waited for the rescuers. They would need their strength in the morning to climb aboard the rescue vessels. So the hulk of *Neosho* settled down, the horribly cramped men in the whaleboats adjusting themselves as best they could, and riding the heavy sea, part of the crew constantly on watch, lest they drift away from the side of *Neosho*.

On the port rail, the pharmacists did what they could to make the seriously wounded men comfortable, and shook their heads over Construction Mechanic Second Class Leon Brooks, whose wounds were very severe. They hoped he would make it through the night. For that matter, they hoped they would all make it through the night, until rescue came.

Chapter Ten

Attack!

At Bandoeng, Sergeant Kawakami was finding the war a little tiresome. He was a soldier, and his men were soldiers, and they were relegated to guarding prisoners of war here on Java. He knew the importance of his work, and he would never have considered thinking negatively about his orders, but he would have found it much more reasonable to be at home in Japan or doing more soldierly chores. On the morning of May 8 the garrison was up at dawn, for there was much to be done. In the past few days some important decisions had been reached, and the result was that this camp would become a center for foreign prisoners, while the Indonesians would be freed as soon as possible, if they could be trusted. The prisoners were to be divided into civil and military contingents, and the barracks and stockades had to be cleared of all others, so that the Dutch could be brought in. The war news, as reported by the radio, was all very good, and there was every reason to believe the pacification program was months ahead of schedule and that normal life could soon begin. It was nearly five years since the "China Incident" that had caused the outbreak of the war. The sergeant was much moved when he considered the one hundred thousand casualties the Imperial Army had suffered, but he was also confident that it would soon be over, with Japan victorious. So he turned to his work on this morning of May 8 with good will.

So, too, did the men of carrier *Lexington*, who were called on that morning to make the first search for the Japanese carriers that had been so close by during the night. Lieutenant C.M. Williams, supply officer of the *Lexington*, whose battle station was in the coding room, had the definite feeling that morning that it was going to be "kill or be killed." Few men had gotten much sleep that night before; the tension on the ship was growing hour by hour, Williams had encountered an old friend in the wardroom, a pilot he had known back in those dim distant days at California Tech, and the pilot had stopped to talk.

"You know how I feel, Charlie?" he asked, as the two paced the deck to walk off their dinner. "Just like the night before a big football game, a football game I've got to win."

That was the old college spirit, the Winsocki spirit, as epitomized in a popular college fight song that was sweeping the nation that spring, a revulsion against the despair and loss of the past few months, and an indication, in its simplest, strictly American terms, of the determination of these navy men to win a battle.

The pilots of *Lexington* were up well before dawn, and briefed on their mission. Admiral Fletcher was concerned, because the shore-based aircraft on which he had been depending had not sighted the Japanese carriers. He thought there might be two of them, but on the other hand there might be three of them out there somewhere—and it was imperative that he strike. Admiral Fitch agreed. He would have tactical control of the force, Fletcher had decided. In fact, Fletcher had decided that Fitch, as the airman, should have tactical control all the way along, but somehow the word had not gotten to Fitch until this day.

If they were to find the Japanese, and they were anywhere within striking distance, there was only one way to do it. They must launch a search around the compass, which meant that every one of those three hundred and sixty degrees must be covered in a great circle extending out hundreds of miles from the carrier. Fitch sent the fliers out by themselves. Usually the pilots went in pairs, it was safer that way, and it probably made for more careful search, but today there was no chance of doing the job quickly enough if they paired up, so the lonely tasks began. At 0530 the clanging of the bell announced the takeoff of the search missions, and the call to general quarters.

Just after midnight Admiral Fitch radioed Fletcher that he wanted the boys to go out 200 miles to the north in the semicircle, and only 125 miles to the south, where the Japanese would seem much less likely to have strayed. Fighter and anti-torpedo patrols should be in the air fifteen minutes before sunrise.

Fifteen minutes later he had his answer.

"As usual I agree with you thoroughly. I will change course to west. Set your own course and speed ..."

So Admiral Fitch was in control, as dawn neared.

The searches launched, the men of *Lexington* and the ships settled down to wait. The general quarters order was secured, and the ship turned to routine matters.

The ship's medical officers passed the word that since they might well be going into battle that morning, it would be wise for every man to put on clean clothes with long-sleeved shirts, to protect them from bomb blast. Lieutenant Williams went up to his deck, showered and shaved and carefully picked up the pay list for the squadrons and his cash book and other valuables and wrapped them up in a package, then put rubber bands on them, so he could grab them and run if need be. He changed his clothes, and went topside. His battle station had been the coding room, but he was ordered now to radio repair where he would be a standby for the coding board in case a bomb wiped out the whole coding room.

Radio repair was a blind compartment, and it was very boring at such an exciting moment to sit there and not be able to see what was going on up deck. So Williams got permission of the officer in charge of his battle station to go out on deck and spot for the anti-aircraft battery pocket halfway down from the deck to the water. It was good to be outside, and he had a feeling that he was going to be able to see what happened.

For two hours nothing happened. On the bridge and in fighter control, radio crackled with the comments and wise cracks of the pilots as they masked their deadly and serious job in small talk. Then, at 0820, Lieutenant Joseph Smith, flying a Scout 2-S-2 saw something below him, took another good look, and radioed excitedly back to the carrier.

The routine traffic that marks a busy task force at sea was interrupted, and *Lexington* called up *Yorktown*. Lieutenant Smith had spotted two carriers, four cruisers and three destroyers, but *Lexington* did not yet know his position, and was frantically trying to raise him again.

It was *Yorktown*, not *Lexington*, that heard the next message, which placed the force at 120 miles away, almost due northeast. And three minutes later, Admiral Fletcher knew that the American task force had been sighted by the Japanese, who had been searching as hard for the enemy as had *Lexington's* pilots.

Admiral Takagi had spent the night steaming north, to provide the air protection that the Port Moresby force felt it needed. Before sunrise Admiral Hara had launched his search planes. One of them had found the Americans at about the time the Americans had found *Shokaku* and *Zuikaku*.

This day, the luck of weather was with the Japanese, not the Americans. The Japanese force was in the cover of a cold front, which meant foul weather and plenty of cloud to hide the ships below. The Americans had moved out of that area, and into pure, bright sunlight, in which the majestic lines of the carriers were starkly limned against the blue of the sea.

Hara followed a different tack than the Americans: while his searches were out, he launched an attack force of 90 planes. It was risky. If the searchers did not find the American carriers and headed off on a wild goose chase, they might be immobilized for hours, at a critical period, and even lost. But it was also bold.

With the word that the Japanese were at last in view, the pilots of the two American carriers rushed to their ready rooms, donning their flight clothes as they went. Deck crews began warming up the engines of the fighters and bombers. Then came the order through the ships, to dog down the watertight doors, and shut the hatches.

There was some confusion. Lieutenant Smith could not be raised again and when Commander Robert Dixon, who was flying the next segment, came over to take a look, it was some time before he found the Japanese ships beneath the murky clouds and heavy rain in the area.

At 0838 it was all clarified and Admiral Fitch signalled for the launch of the entire striking group, including the torpedo planes. Half an hour later Admiral Fletcher ran up a signal on *Yorktown*: he was passing tactical control to Admiral Fitch for the battle to come.

Fletcher's action was wise and foresighted. Fitch was an old-line aviator, and a very competent one. He had graduated from the naval academy in 1906, served in battleships and destroyers. He was forty-seven years old before he took aviation training, but since that time he had served continuously in the air arm, as commander of the carrier *Langley*, commander of Patrol Wing Two, commander of Carrier Division One with his flag in *Saratoga*. Now he was commander of the Air Task Force in the Pacific, and responsible for the management of the planes and the carriers. Fletcher could not have been better served than to have Fitch in control.

Above the Japanese task force Commander Dixon stayed put, circling around, giving positions and waiting for the American fleet of planes that was supposed to arrive soon. He was, at that moment, living a very dangerous life. The Japanese combat air patrol quickly discovered his presence, and the Zeros came up to chase him. Dixon was an old hand, he was the commanding officer of Scouting Squadron Two, and had been in aviation ever since academy days when he stayed over after June Week for a summer course in aviation, then took flight training after a brief tour with the fleet.

He began ducking in and out of the cloud cover, his rear gunner craning his eyes and warning of the approach of any of the flashing Zeros. The Japanese were wary, they saw that rear gun mount and they tried to get the gunner to exhaust his ammunition so they could sweep in for a kill. But Dixon's gunner would not play—he followed the Zeros as they came around, but did not fire until they were within range. And coming within range was something they did not just then want to do very badly. Dixon turned and climbed and kept in the clouds, heading toward the Japanese planes if they came too close, and then kiting away from them. For two hours and more he held this position, waiting for the attack to arrive.

Yorktown's planes got away first. At 0924 the carrier launched 24 dive bombers, six fighters, and nine torpedo bombers. They flew in the direction indicated by Commander Dixon, and prepared to attack. *Lexington* launched ten minutes later, putting up 24 bombers, ten fighters, and 12 torpedo planes.

Even as the American planes got away, Captain Frederick Sherman of Lexington was telling his officers to be ready for a Japanese attack at about 11 o'clock that morning. He had intercepted a Japanese report giving the course and speed and location of the American task force, and he knew it would not be very long before his enemy would arrive.

The American attack group arrived over the Japanese carriers, or at least *Yorktown's* dive bombers did. These planes were led by two fighters, which kept their eyes out for Japanese planes. The bombers began to circle at 17,000 feet, and await the arrival of the slow, lumbering torpedo planes. The weather was "unsettled," as the pilots called it, with rain squalls standing up from the sea here and there and a broken layer of clouds at 2000 feet that helped obscure the movements of the Japanese task force below.

Seeing the Americans above, Admiral Hara began taking protective action. *Zuikaku* headed for a rain squall, while *Shokaku* headed into the wind and began launching planes—an augmented force for her combat air patrol, to deal with the enemy planes above. The Japanese cruisers and destroyers, moved around the ships in a fan shaped formation, which they often used for defense, and opened up at long range with their anti-aircraft guns. The battle was joined.

At 1058 the torpedo planes arrived, twenty-six minutes after the dive bombers. For some pilots this twenty-six minutes delay would mean the difference between getting home and not getting home again, but that was a matter for Washington to worry about. Now the important task was to attack and the dive bombers got ready to peel off.

Lexington's planes were well behind; she seemed jinxed this morning. On takeoff one of the four fighters assigned to the protection of the dive bombers, was damaged when another plane ran into its tail and the propeller chewed out a piece of it, so that pilot's mission was scratched. That left three fighters to protect Commander William Ault's attack force of dive bombers, four with the command force of scout bombers, and two others to protect the torpedo bombers. But three fighters, and the dive bombers, got lost from their charges' vicinity, and halfway through the mission came home, for their job could not be finished. And then, Lex's torpedo squadron arrived at the position discussed in the very earliest report, and found nothing there, so had to begin flying a box-pattern search, wasting valuable time in order to find the Japanese. The dive bombers got lost finally, never did find the Japanese carriers, and returned to the task force when their gasoline supply became critical.

Lieutenant Commander Joe Taylor's torpedo squadron led the Yorktown attack. The idea was to hit them high and hit them low: the torpedo planes to come in low from the southeast in this case, while the dive bombers came down from 17,000 feet. Thus the attention of the 18 Zero fighters the Japanese seemed to have in the air would be split, and the slow torpedo bombers would have a better chance of survival.

Who ever thought that Joe Taylor, born in the year that Admiral Fitch had graduated from the naval academy, would one day be peering through the windshield of his TBD, lining up a big Japanese carrier to try to sink her? Taylor was one of the new breed: his whole naval career had been wrapped up in aviation, almost from the day he left Danville, Illinois, high school and headed for the sprawling campus on the Severn, where naval officers were made. Ensign Taylor graduated and was commissioned in 1927, then stayed on for aviation training and was assigned that same year to help fit out the *Lexington* after she was launched. He had served in her for a year before taking flight training, which meant he was a sea-going officer as well as a pilot, and after he had his wings, he had again gone to *Lex*, as a pilot in the scouting squadron. For a year and a half he flew big flying boats, as a member of Patrol Squadron 4, based at Pearl Harbor, then he was assigned as a float plane pilot to the cruiser *Astoria* when she was commissioned. A tour with Fighting 1, the squadron assigned to *Langley*, completed a well-rounded experience, then a year of hard work, as a test pilot with the experimental division of the Norfolk naval air station, two years with dive bombers, and here he was in a torpedo plane. With four engagements behind him: the raid on the Gilberts and Marshalls of February, the raid on Salamaua and Lae after the Japanese occupied them in March, the Tulagi raid, and yesterday's sinking of *Shoho*, Lieutenant Commander Taylor was now one of the handful of most experienced combat pilots in the American naval air force; the cream of the crop, so to speak.

Taylor's nine torpedo planes were split into three divisions, and as the dive bombers began attacking, they approached. To avoid the coming dives, the *Shokaku* turned hard a-port, and then reversed, hard a-starboard, creating a lovely S to mark where she had been. As she turned right, Taylor's planes moved, each division reaching an attack point, and heading toward the enemy, whereupon the formation broke up and each pilot attacked in his own way. As they ran in, the ships before them began opening up with anti-aircraft fire, and *Shokaku* put up a virtual barrage.

Lieutenant Commander William O. Burch Jr. led his dive bombers down from their perch at 17,000 feet, and right behind him came Ensign J.H. Jorgenson. They dropped to 2500 feet, and watched *Shokaku*'s wake create that big S as they came. Jorgenson saw Burch's bomb hit the deck of the carrier, amidships, near the island. Then he was too busy to see much, for some of *Shokaku*'s gunners were concentrating on the dive bombers, and his plane was hit as he reached down to close his diving flaps.

The dive bomber shuddered and lurched, and fell into a spin off to the left. Jorgenson pulled out, and saw that a shell had ripped through his left aileron and wing, tearing off the protective fabric, and making the plane a little sluggish to fly. That was nearly disastrous, for just then three Zeros came after this cripple, shooting. Bullets tore away the telescopic sight, clanged against the armored back of his seat. (If he had been in a Zero he would have been dead.) Other shots angled into the cockpit, breaking the glass and smashing most of his instruments, and one cut the oxygen tube lying on his forearm. Three bullets grazed his right leg and he got a little shrapnel in his foot.

Behind, Jorgenson's gunner was peppering the Japanese, and he shot one plane down, but three more came charging in from dead ahead, and then Jorgenson began pumping his own guns, and had the satisfaction of seeing one Japanese fighter turn away, smoking.

The cream of the American crop was meeting the cream of the Japanese crop, for these pilots of *Shokaku* and *Zuikaku* were among the most experienced of the war. They had fought at the very beginning in the Pearl Harbor raid. Jorgenson was very lucky to escape the fighters, but he pulled into a cloud, and as he came out found a group of his fellows. He tagged along, Radiomangunner Brunetti scanning the skies behind them as they headed for home.

Lieutenant Commander Burch circled, led his men into the cover of a big cumulous cloud, and then watched as well as he could to see the hits on the carrier. He counted six and three more probables. There would have been better shooting, he said later, if they had not been dogged again by the fogging of the windshields of the dive bombers as they went down from high. Now he knew that this happened every time they tried to attack in anything but perfect clear weather—and of course the reason it had not been discovered before combat was that the war games had usually been played in fine weather.

Burch headed home, too, noting that the Japanese fighters were doing their job well—they attacked the planes as they came in and out. But once the Americans joined up to go home, the Zeros lost interest and turned to other enemies of their ship who had yet to attack. The bombers, said Burch, had accounted for 11 Japanese fighters in those few minutes, with another nine damaged.

Joe Taylor's pilots dropped their nine torpedoes, and were astounded at the results. He estimated, later, that at least three of them had hit home, and three others unfortunately made erratic runs, which indicated something wrong in the mechanism or the dropping. But he was gratified with what he saw:

The last two pilots of the Torpedo Squadron to attack stated that the first torpedo struck the port bow and laid it open from the waterline to the flight deck. The second and third torpedoes hit between the bow and the midships section. The area on the port side from the bow aft for about 50 to 100 feet was one mass of flames from the waterline to the flight deck. The flame was exceptionally intense. It looked like that from an acetylene torch, and appeared to be coming from inside the ship. Another small fire was burning at the starboard quarter. When the carrier was last seen, about fifteen minutes after the attack, the fires were burning fiercely. It is believed probable that this carrier was so badly damaged that it finally sank.

Those nine torpedo planes were escorted by four of the fighters, and right there in the middle of the fight were the two who had been pulled out of Guadalcanal three days earlier, Lieutenant McCuskey and Ensign Adams. The fighters were up at 2000 feet, to keep an umbrella over the torpedo planes as they came in low, just off the water. They watched as the Japanese cruisers gave them demonstration of a trick they had never before seen: as the torpedo planes came in, the cruisers fired their big guns into the water ahead of them, creating a waterspout, and hoping the TBD's would run into one, and crash.

But Joe Taylor and his boys came on in, and a

moment later, McCuskey, Adams, and Lieutenants Leonard and Woolen were too busy to watch the demonstration any further. The Zeros were coming down. So the F4F's went up, and soon the air was filled, it seemed, with roiling, slipping planes, firing bursts of bullets at one another, and occasionally one would hesitate, smoke, and burst into flames, or spin into the sea. The American tactics were effective. The four fighters drove off the Japanese, so that all nine torpedo planes were able to make their drops. Considering the speed of the TBS, the speed of the Zero, and the fact that McCuskey and his friends were outnumbered, it was not a bad job at all, and in doing it they claimed to have shot down three fighters and one Japanese scout bomber.

In a few minutes, the *Yorktown* pilots' attack was over and they headed back toward their carrier, before the *Lexington* planes ever found the Japanese force.

Yorktown's pilots had left *Shokaku* on fire forward and severely damaged, and when Admiral Hara aboard *Zuikaku* emerged from his rain squall at the end of the attack, he saw his carrier blazing. But by the time the *Lexington* pilots arrived at about 1140, apparently the fires had been put out, for *Lexington*'s Group commander Ault and his fliers thought they saw an undamaged carrier before them. In fact, they saw two carriers, both undamaged as far as they could see.

The weather down on the deck had been very poor, so Lieutenant Commander James H. Brett Jr.'s torpedo bombers had come up to 6000 feet. Here, finding a hole in the clouds that covered the Japanese task force, they spiralled down to attack. The Japanese Zeros were after them, all eleven of them, and the fighter pilots zoomed in to confront the Japanese—four U.S. fighters.

Twelve torpedo bombers had set out, but *Lex*'s bad luck this day held, and one had to turn back with oil-pressure trouble. Now the other eleven and the fighters had more trouble than that—for the angry Japanese pilots were upon them. The fighters sped to seek the enemy, there were more than the eighteen in the air who had met the men of *Yorktown*, and the Americans fought fiercely. Lieutenant Noel Gayler, one of them, said he saw his comrades each "get" at least one Zero—but then the other three American fighters were shot down. Two of them went into the sea without a word, but Ensign H.F. Clark managed to fly away with his damaged plane, and last heard of that day was announcing that he was getting ready to ditch.

Gayler shot down one Zero as the Japanese pilot tried to lure him into a climb—for the Zero was notably faster and more maneuverable than the F4F, and nowhere more than in a climb. The Japanese pilot, climbing, could outdistance his enemy, flop over and be on him in a moment. A live pilot did not climb with Zeros. Gayler shot, was lucky, rolled and went into a cloud. That was why he was a live pilot. He ducked out the other side and saw a handful of Zeros waiting; he ducked back in and came out at another angle, and the reception committee was there again. The cloud, as he said, became his "home away from home" and he stayed in it, peeking out from time to time. Always the Zeros were there. Finally he burst out the bottom of his cloud and down below was a Zero, just in the position F4F's liked best. He nosed over, the Japanese pilot pulled up, and moved right in front of the F4F's guns. Burn one Zero.

The game of hide and seek with Gayler, and the

destruction of his wingmates, gave the *Lexington* torpedo squadron the respite they needed to make their attack, which was combined with the dive bombing of Commander Ault's four planes, the *Lexington* dive bombers never appearing on the scene. Ault called, repeatedly, but he could not raise them, and so he decided to go in alone.

The torpedo planes went in, and they claimed five hits on the carrier. The bombers claimed three, and the pilots spoke of the towering masses of smoke and debris that rose after each bomb struck home. And as they left the scene of the action, they were sure they left behind them a sinking Japanese carrier, settling fast.

But the Japanese were not nearly so badly hurt as the Americans supposed. Admiral Hara came out of his rain squall, watched the *Lexington* force attack, and fired at them. Then he turned his attention to the damage. Cruisers *Kinugasa* and *Furutaka*, which had joined up with the Takagi force after the sinking of *Shoho*, had both been attacked, but neither was hit. *Kinugasa* had been narrowly missed by a bomb from a dive bomber, and the captain of *Furutaka* had been able to turn his ship in time to see a torpedo wake go skimming along the beam. Otherwise no damage.

Shokaku was very seriously damaged, there was no question about that. More than a hundred of her crew had been killed and nearly fifty more wounded. She had big holes in her deck and in her sides, and below there were fires and planes and equipment had been twisted and burned. But she had no holes below the waterline, which meant they could salvage her if they were lucky—and she could at least operate well enough to get undamaged planes off and over to *Zuikaku*. Admiral Takagi considered the problem, and decided that *Shokaku* would have to be gotten out of these waters immediately. There was no naval facility closer than Japan that could handle the extensive damage she had received; she was lucky to be afloat. So deciding, he made the signals, and *Shokaku*, with escorting destroyers, was dispatched toward the Land of the Rising Sun.

Meanwhile, the Japanese combat air patrol from the two carriers was chasing the American attack force from *Lexington* on its way home. It was not an easy chase, for the Americans had stingers in their tails in the twin machine guns that every torpedo bomber carried. The leader, Commander Brett, made sure they stayed in tight formation, for thus was their defense power improved mightily. The Japanese followed them, attacked, and were driven off by eleven pairs of after guns. They circled around, then attacked again, and the gunners shot down the leader of the formation. Another leader took his place, and the Japanese planes changed their attack and came in from the port quarter. The guns blazed again, and the leader fell into the sea. The rest of the Zeros turned then, and headed home, while the torpedo planes kept moving toward *Lexington*.

Now it was not the Japanese but the sea that beset them the sea and its wind and weather. Getting back was going to be a problem, Brett could see, because they had used up so much fuel in their long search for the Japanese after the information they had worked on was proved to be wrong.

Brett told his pilots to lean their mixture, which cut down power, but made up for it in longevity. They took advantage of the air, trimming for best flight.

Commander Ault and his three companion dive bombers were unhurt by the anti-aircraft fire and managed to avoid the fighters on their run in. They climbed back up to meet their fighter escort and started home, too. But the Zeros, which had turned away from the torpedo planes, now came at these pilots in force. Someone counted more than 20 enemy fighters. The F4F's—only two of them—headed in to meet the enemy, and in a few minutes both American fighters were shot down. The Japanese now went after the dive bombers, and dropped them one by one. Commander Ault's plane was badly damaged, and his gunner was severely wounded. Another pass by Zeros, and the engine of the SBD began to cough; he radioed back to *Lexington* that he might have to make a forced landing at sea.

So the American strike was ended, with *Shokaku* limping away, and Admiral Hara gathering his planes together on *Zuikaku* and listening, to discover what the Japanese strike force was doing at the other end of the scene.

As Admiral Fletcher had put it at the beginning of this day, the contest would determine the control of the air and the fate of the Port Moresby invasion force. Success would strengthen Japan immeasurably in the South Pacific. Failure would mean the very first halt in the roll of the Japanese juggernaut across the western hemisphere.

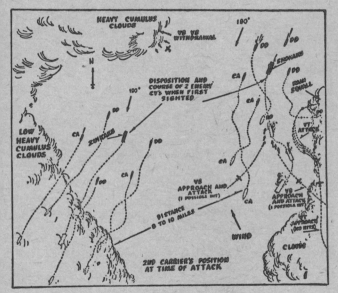

Attack on the *Shokaku*, 8 May

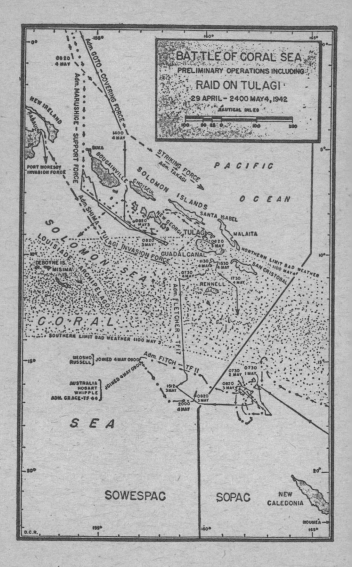

Chapter Eleven

Hara's Counterattack

While the planes of *Yorktown* were attacking *Shokaku* and even before the planes of *Lexington* found the enemy task force, the Japanese were striking *Lexington* and *Yorktown*. The Japanese were luckier and more skilful than the Americans, for their planes followed the American scouts back to the carriers, and they wasted no time in fruitless search, nor did any large group get lost.

For at least an hour the combat air patrol and the anti-torpedo patrol planes had investigated various reports of "bogeys" that came up on the radar screens of the two ships.

At 1014 the combat air patrol shot down a Japanese float plane, and then the formations were tightened as the Americans got ready to take the coming attack.

Admiral Fitch changed the course of the task force to 28° at 1030, in order to make shorter the distance the American pilots would have to fly from their attack. He knew they would be coming home short of gas, that some would be wounded, that some planes would be wobbling from gunshot. The force moved on at 15 knots, cutting the distance a little every moment. The ships moved on. Fifteen minutes later Fitch ordered the cruisers to their defensive pattern around the carriers. Then, at 1055, radar reported many aircraft coming in from the north, just as Joe

Taylor told Bill Burch over the radio that he was moving in against *Shokaku.*

Lexington launched the rest of her combat air patrol and the fighter director gave the call that alerted every American pilot in the air:

"Hey Rube."

It was the old circus cry for help, that meant every plane in the air should come to the help of the carriers. *Yorktown* sent out an additional alert to its antitorpedo plane patrol, warning of a large enemy force some 45 miles off, moving at a rate of about three miles a minute.

Yorktown had been at general quarters since 0545, when the first planes were preparing to launch. The ship control party was on the "island"; Captain Buckmaster at the conn on the navigation bridge, and in the pilot house. He was assisted by three officers. One of them stood by to see that orders to the engine main control were understood and immediately carried out. The captain knew that the carriers would be the main targets of the Japanese attack when it came, and that his ability to maneuver the ship might mean the difference between a safe ship and a sunk one. There must be no human error, no slipup in reporting or obeying orders, and no failure in communications if it could be avoided.

The other two officers on the bridge at the service of the captain were assigned to the port and starboard wings and they were his lookouts, helping him spot enemy planes as they came in, and reporting on their movements and apparent intentions.

Commander I.D. Wiltsie, the navigator, was stationed in the conning tower, where he attended to the steering, main engine, and whistle controls. Captain Buckmaster's procedure was to give his orders to the navigator, as they regarded the main engines and rudder. He spoke through the conning tower slits, and then duplicated the orders by talking on the battle-telephone circuit. Commander Dixie Kiefer, the executive officer, was stationed in Battle II, which was at the after end of the bridge level platform, 120 feet from the pilot house. His task was to maintain ship and crew, and to repair damage, while the captain conned, and the chief engineer kept her going.

When the enemy began coming in, Captain Buckmaster asked Captain Sherman of *Lexington* to move a little, and *Yorktown* changed position so that *Lexington* would not be in her sun—that is so that Japanese planes, which could be expected to head in out of the sun, would be visible to *Yorktown*'s gunners. The captain also eased off the alert condition enough to start the ventilation blowers, which had been shut down for hours. The ship was growing foul below decks and men were standing by the opening panting for breath. That was no way to start a battle. While the Japanese came in, but while they were still out, the captain aired the ship. But only for three minutes. Then the blowers were stopped, and the *Yorktown* got ready to take an attack. The Japanese were less than thirty miles away, coming fast.

Between 1102 and 1104 Captain Buckmaster launched four more fighters, and at that point all the carrier's serviceable planes were in the air.

The waiting was hard. At 1106 the radar showed the planes at 29 miles, and minute by minute they moved in. At 1111 they were 15 miles off, and were now recognized as torpedo planes. Captain Buckmaster changed course to 125°, in response to Admiral Fitch's order, speed now 20 knots. One minutes later the speed was increased to flank speed, which for *Yorktown* was 25 knots.

The wind was coming from the northeast, at about 16 knots. The sea was relatively smooth. Visibility, unfortunately for the carrier, was perfect up to 30 miles. Admirals Fletcher and Fitch would have given a lot, right then, for a nice big rain squall.

Six miles out, the Japanese torpedo planes began sorting themselves out, and it was apparent that they would divide to attack both carriers, that the attacks of dive bombers and torpedo planes would be simultaneous—good carrier doctrine, as practiced by the Americans that very morning.

Above the carriers, the combat air patrol of eight fighters was very low on fuel, which was bound to create a problem. Nine more fighters were launched, but the force was very short, on fighters, and so dive bombers were used to do fighter work. By the time the Japanese attack materialized, there were 23 of these in the air. Here is the way it was, as reported on the figher circuit at the beginning of the battle. *Lexington*'s fighter section consisted of four two-lane divisions—Doris Red, Doris White, Agnes White, and Agnes Red, which had three planes. *Yorktown*'s fighters were designated Wildcat Red, Blue, Orange, and Brown.

The five planes of Agnes Red and White were vectored out northeast, 20 miles away at an altitude (Angels) of 10,000 feet. Agnes Red made contact with the enemy force at that point but the three pilots found they were two thousand feet below the Japanese planes, and in no position to attack. One pilot radioed back that there were fifty to sixty planes in the flight, stacked in layers, extending from 10,000 feet up to 13,000 feet. A third of them, he said, were fighters, and they were up top. Down below them were the dive bombers. Then came another level of

112

fighters, which protected the torpedo bombers, flying lowest of all.

The three planes of Agnes Red climbed to attack. Meanwhile the two planes of *Lexington's* Agnes White fighter section, were sent down low to intercept the torpedo planes of an advance group. (The Japanese attacked with sixty-nine planes altogether, not all of them in that big wave.)

Here is the way it was, as reported on the fighter circuit at the beginning of the battle:

1114 From *Lexington*:	Our planes have sighted enemy and are going after them.
1115 Romeo (*Lexington*):	What are Angels? High 9 to 10. Those fighters over us now on right hand side over you on your port side.
1115 *Yorktown* to CTG 17.5 (Fitch) and *Lexington*	Launched 4 VF (fighters) combat air patrol Red Blue at 1103.
1116	Come over here and join Marin and I, on our port side.
Brown to Romeo:	Dead ahead, bearing 100 (The enemy)
To Romeo:	Agnes White has a torpedo plane. (one of the anti-torpedo patrol was after a Japanese plane)
1117	Come on Wildcats, let's get up (A call from the fighter leader to the *Yorktown* planes to gain altitude for an attack.)
1119 Wildcat (*Yorktown*) planes	Keep a sharp lookout for torpedo planes.

113

The Japanese were now boring in and the dive bombers serving as anti-torpedo planes made a valiant effort to stop them.

Eight Douglas SBDs pushed in to try to knock out the Japanese. They were immediately bounced by Japanese Zero fighters, and four of the eight were shot down in short order. But the SBDs did shoot down four dive bombers, too—so it was not a waste, in terms of the effort.

As the attack opened, the anti-aircraft guns of the carriers and the support ships began to fire. Nothing smaller than five-inch was effective at this range, but in a few moments the Japanese were in close enough for the smaller guns to begin popping.

The torpedo planes were approaching from the port beam, but when they divided, several moved around to starboard of the carriers. Then they came in to drop. Three planes dropped torpedoes on the port quarter of *Yorktown*; four others came in from the port beam. When the first torpedo struck the water, Captain Buckmaster moved:

"Full right rudder," he ordered. "*Emergency* flank speed." This meant the engine room was to give the ship every bit of power it had—take it up to thirty knots.

This maneuver, plus maneuvering by *Lexington*, took the carriers apart, and split the force of protective ships. *Yorktown* was now surrounded by cruisers *Astoria, Portland,* and *Chester,* and destroyers *Russell, Hammann, and Aylwin.* They stood out 2000 yards from the carrier, and shot at the Japanese as they came in, putting up a very heavy barrage that obviously disturbed the Japanese attack.

Captain Buckmaster now began a brilliant defensive effort, maneuvering the carrier furiously; "violent maneuvers, the most radical I saw during the war," said Commander Elliot W. Shanklin, gunnery officer of the *Astoria*, who observed it all from his post a mile away.

The laconic battle report of Captain Buckmaster gives the skeleton of the story:

> The ship was steadied on a course parallel to the second three torpedoes sufficiently long to allow them to run past the port side close aboard. The planes in these groups had been under continuous fire by all ships in their vicinity. Four were seen shot down from the first group, but three drops were completed. Of the planes which had been on the port beam, one plane was set afire and crashed after dropping torpedo and another dove into the water before dropping. The torpedoes of the first group were not observed close to the ship.

The Japanese had gotten in past the scanty fighter cover and the SBDs, and although the bombers had fought hard, and damaged a good number of the Japanese fighters, they were badly shot up, too, and several were trying to limp home to their carriers.

Yorktown's fighters, Wildcat Red and Wildcat Blue sections, were sent out to the northeast, 15 miles, at an altitude of 1000 feet, to intercept torpedo planes. But by the time they arrived at that point, the Japanese had passed in through it, and the fighters found nothing. Fighter control then directed them to climb to 10,000 feet: Wildcat Red leader called the *Lex.*

1119 Wildcat Red Leader to Romeo:	I am at 10,000 feet astern from ship. Give me something to do.
Romeo:	Return to ship. It is being attacked.

115

| Red Leader: | Do you mean return over ship? |

But just then fighter control broke off to issue a general call:

| From *Lexington*: | Warning aircraft bearing 130 25 miles from Orange. Warning, enemy bombers protected by 9 fighters. |

Then fighter control came back to his conversation with Red Leader:

| 1120 Romeo to Red Leader: | As quick as possible. We are being attacked by torpedo planes and everything. |

A moment later, Brown Leader was on the air.

| 1121 Brown Leader to Brown Two. Up: | Angels 10 (10,000 feet) Join |

The SBDs of the anti-torpedo patrol had been outdistanced by the faster enemy, and now wanted to get back into the fight.

| 1121 Commander Anti Torpedo Patrol to *Yorktown*: | Where are the torpedo planes coming from? |
| *Yorktown*: | From our port beam. There appears to be no particular concentration. |

But just at that moment, the air action grew hot:

1122   Just behind you! Just behind you!
1123   Bandits, enemy fighters down here. Let's go. I can't find my way. I'm tailing behind you.

1125   Bandits turning to 170 all around. Bandits are closing in. Bandits are closing in. Bandits 170 five to ten.

1127   From Agnes: Enemy dead astern, 10 (degrees.) What altitude?
Angels 17. I do not see the bandits. I am 8 miles.

Just then, *Yorktown*'s radar chose to go out of commission. Captain Buckmaster tried to inform *Lexington* on the fighter circuit, but got no answer.

Wildcat to Romeo	Radar out.
Wildcat to Romeo	Acknowledge (No answer)
1134 Brown Leader to Romeo	12 miles west of you. Angels 12. Request instructions.

Red Two was in trouble.

Red Two to Red Leader:	Engine is going out. I'm going to make forced landing in water.

But it was obvious that while she was under attack, *Lexington*'s fighter control circuit had broken down, too, and there was no answer from *Lexington*. *Yorktown* took over direction.

Wildcat to all planes in air:	Wildcat radar out. Protect the force.
Red Two to Wildcat:	I am making a forced landing. Directly in front of you. (Red Two, badly damaged in the air fight, was ditching.)
Wildcat to Red Two:	Good Luck.

117

Now other fighters came on the air, indicating the fury of the battle up above the carriers.

Wildcat Brown to Romeo: Pancake guns. (I want to land for ammunition.)

Orange leader to Wildcat: Request permission to land aboard. Hurt. Acknowledge.

Wildcat to Orange leader: Permission granted. Land aboard.

Brown leader, unable to raise *Lexington* fighter control, addressed himself to his own carrier.

1137 Brown to Wildcat: Request permission to pancake. Guns.

Wildcat to Brown leader: Permission granted.

All this while, Captain Buckmaster had been zigging and zagging his ship in a pattern that made the support ships' task of protection very difficult, and yet the cruisers and the destroyers kept right with *Yorktown*; not one fell off station. The torpedo planes that came in the second wave against *Yorktown* rounded the stern about five miles out and attacked from the starboard quarter, but Captain Buckmaster turned hard left, presented the stern of the ship to the enemy, a narrow target, and opened up with the guns. The Japanese planes dropped their torpedoes a long way out, which gave the ship more chance to avoid them, and then one of the torpedo bombers splashed into the sea. Two torpedoes were seen running down the starboard side of the ship.

Even the Americans were impressed with the performance of one particular torpedo plane. This Japanese pilot made his approach parallel to the starboard beam of the ship, to a point forward. All the way in, coming at 200 knots, with his torpedo, the

118

plane was under heavy fire from the five-inch guns and the smaller anti-aircraft weapons. He turned towards the ship and every gun was trained on him. In he came to 2000 yards, and then dropped his torpedo, and spiraled off in a perfect left chandelle. Captain Buckmaster had turned the ship toward the torpedo as it was dropped, and so it ran across the bow, but it was a very near thing. A few more Japanese pilots with such tenacity and *Yorktown* would be in trouble.

The trouble came in the form of dive bombers. They moved in over the formation at 1124 and headed for *Yorktown* from out of the sun, aiming for the bridge and the island, in general. Captain Buckmaster began dealing with this new threat; the technique was to lead into the direction of the diving plane, with rudder hard over, as the dive bomber came.

Part of the secret of *Yorktown*'s effective defense this day was the captain's alertness. Part of it was the effectiveness of cooperation with the navigator, Commander Wiltsie. And part of it was the swiftness with which Captain Buckmaster's aides relayed information to him.

Lieutenant (jg) John F. Greenbacker, officer of the deck, was stationed on the starboard wing of the bridge, and he reported constantly on the approach of enemy planes. Lieutenant (jg) C.B. Gill stood on the port wing and did the same. Ensign N.L. Tate was stationed at the alidade on the starboard wing and gave the true bearings of the approaching planes, while Chief Earnest E. Parton did the same on the port wing. The teamwork was flawless and it showed.

At 1124 one dive bomber began his swoop and was seen from the sun sector on the port beam. Four five-inch guns opened up, and so did three 1-inch guns, 12 twenty-millimeter guns, and fourteen 150-calibre guns. For the next four minutes *Yorktown* was a very busy ship. Eighteen planes attacked, two dived on *Lexington*, then climbed to 2000 feet and dived on *Yorktown*, perhaps strafing after they had bombed. Fourteen of the dive bombers dropped bombs intended for *Yorktown*, and they were very good bombers, for there were twelve very near misses, and one bomb fell about 300 yards off the port beam, when its carrying plane lost a wing to *Yorktown* anti-aircraft fire. Four other dive bombers were shot down in this attack. One bomb, dropped at 1127, hit the ship.

A single bomb, hitting a great ship like a carrier, would not seem to have caused much of a problem—yet any bomb could sink a ship, as the war had already shown in the deaths of the *Repulse* and *Prince of Wales* at the beginning of the war, and as the sinking of the carrier *Princeton* by a single 500-pound bomb would show later. This bomb that hit *Yorktown* was a delayed-action armor-piercing type of about 800 pounds, just 12 inches in diameter. The bomber came down to 1500 feet at a 60-degree angle and dropped. His aim was true, and the bomb struck the flight deck, six feet starboard of the centerline of the ship. That deck was steel plate covered by three inches of pine; it did not even slow down the bomb, which bent the plating inward, and went through the gallery deck, doing the same. It went through the hangar, smashing into the first, then the second, then the third deck, and exploding there in the aviation storeroom, fifty feet inside the bowels of the ship.

That fourth deck was armored with 1.5 inches of steel and the bomb did not penetrate further but dished the deck downward for an area of 40 square feet. A hole six feet around was blown in the third deck, and around it the deck was burned and peeled for 35 square feet. The blast effect went back to the second deck, blowing a hole four feet in diameter, and blowing the scuttle off a hatch. The hangar deck, two decks up from the blast, was bulged up, and one hatch was blown out of its dogs. Still, from the flight deck all anyone could see was one relatively small hole.

Down below, the blast destroyed the forward engine-room access trunk, blew off one bulkhead of the laundry, smashed a watertight door, and blew another apart, and threw a large cover fifteen feet into the No. 2 elevator pit. It wrecked the ship's service store, and the soda fountain equipment, the laundry issue room, the ship's service office, the engineer's office, and played havoc in one of the compartments where the ship's marines bunked.

Splinters of jagged metal flew out in all directions after the blast, but were largely blunted by steel walls. But the bomb did start fires. One began immediately after the blast in the rags and target sleeves in the storeroom. The flash caused a fire in the paint above the bomb hole on the hangar deck, but luckily did not ignite paint stored in other compartments.

The explosion also produced dense black smoke and gas. The bomb had broken the intake valves from three firerooms, and these filled with smoke so that the men inside had to abandon them.

On deck, it had all come so fast, no one was quite sure what had happened. At almost this same moment, came three near misses on the starboard quarter that lifted the ship and raised the screws clear of the water. At least two of the near misses sent shrapnel flying across the ship, and the noise and confusion were so great that some lookouts were reporting more torpedo planes attacking, when what they saw were planes moving away after dropping their bombs.

The smoke pouring into Number 9 fireroom, caused someone to raise the fire alarm. It was understandable; the bomb had knocked out all the lights, the room was full of gas and smoke, and the burners, hit by concussion, suffered a flareback that looked very much as though the ship was erupting in flames. The engineers secured boilers Number 8 and Number 9 and ordered abandonment of the rooms. Number 7 boiler had to be shut down, too.

On the bridge, Captain Buckmaster was concerned; it could be desperate if the ship lost power during the bombing. And what if there were another wave?

What speed was available? he asked Lieutenant Commander J.F. Delaney, the engineering officer.

Twenty four knots, said the engineer.

The captain knew that two boilers were out and that two condensers had been immobilized with salt water. Should he slow the ship? he asked.

"Hell no! We'll make it." said Lieutenant Commander Delaney.

What the commander did not tell the bridge was the tragedy that had befallen the engineer's repair party, and the very close escape Delaney had from death himself. The bomb exploded in the compartment directly over Delaney's head as he stood at his action station, and virtually wiped out his repair crew.

Lieutenant Milton E. Ricketts was in charge of the repair party. When the bomb passed through that compartment, he was badly wounded. He pulled himself up from the deck, and looked around. All his men were down, dead, wounded or knocked out by the blast, and a fire was breaking out. He dragged himself forward, opened the valve of the fire plug nearby, led out as much of the fire hose as his strength would allow, and began playing a stream of water on the fire. Then, as it subsided, he dropped the hose and fell dead.

Carpenter Boyd M. McKenzie, in charge of another repair party, discovered the state of affairs in the engineers' repair party compartment, and made his way into the black-smokefilled space, finding the wounded and directing his men to get them out and to sick bay. He led the fire fighting, to get that blaze extinguished. Boatswain Edmund B. Crosby moved in to supervise fire fighting and the removal of the dead and injured, until the place was clear and Lieutenant Ralph Patterson, the senior repair officer, could report up to the executive officer that the fire was under control.

Down below, Lieutenant Commander Delaney was getting plenty of help in his efforts to keep the ship going at high speed and repair the damaged boilers. Water Tender First Class Raymond C. Davis and Fireman First Class George R. Neilson, Jr. hurried to the scene of the trouble. Neilson jumped into the space where the fire was burning on that deck, and called for a fire hose. He played it on the fire so that Davis could get into boiler rooms eight and nine and check the damage.

Meanwhile Lieutenant (jg) Edward A. Kearney, the junior medical officer, had hurried to the engineering compartment to help the wounded. They were moved to sick bay, to be treated by the doctors and the corpsmen.

Altogether there were sixty-six serious casualties, 40 men killed and 26 seriously wounded, several of whom would die later.

There were other injuries, many of them to men who manned the guns. In the rapid firing, no matter what training Lieutenant Commander Ernest J. Davis had given them in the last few weeks, the guns were subject to stoppages and misfires and the press of action. At Number 5 gun (five-inch) the first shellman very nearly lost his hand. The gun was firing on local control when an order came to shift to director control, and the first shellman tried to remove the shell in the loading tray, which had a fixed fuze setting and thus would not respond to director control. At that moment, Rammerman Charles Vodicka started to ram the load and the shellman's hand was caught between rammer spade and shell. Vodicka saw, and in mid action stopped and retracted the shell, saving his buddy's hand. But the hand was injured, and the first shellman had to head for sick bay. The gun captain made for the platform to help until a replacement could come up, but he was knocked down by a bomb's near miss, and put out of action for a few minutes. First Powerman Raymond Rolfe then loaded both powder and shell and the gun continued to fire without interruption.

At five-inch gun Number 8, Gunner's Mate William H. Newman was firing when the power went out to the rammer motor. He then began loading and ramming by hand. Trainer Wilford Moore was burned, and knocked out of his seat three times by blasts from the gun next to him, but he continued to fight and would not let the captain relieve him.

These were little incidents, small examples that sailors would scarcely call heroism. They were part of the job that day, but they made the difference between a good ship and a fair one, and some one action by one of these men very well may have saved the ship.

By 1135 the brunt of the attack had been expended, and the Japanese were turning away and reforming to head back to their own carriers. *Yorktown* turned into the wind, for up above her planes were asking for permission to come in, low on gas and many of them out of ammunition.

Some of the ship's guns were still firing at Japanese planes, and one torpedo plane was still in the area, not yet having dropped its "fish." Commander Murr Arnold, the air officer, was ready for his "bird," to bring them in and service them. Now the job was Lieutenant N.A. Campbell's. He was the ship's landing officer, and he had to try to bring in planes that were out of gas or badly shot up, and save planes and pilots if he could.

Up above, *Yorktown*'s planes circled, waiting for instructions. *Lexington*'s fighter circuit came back in and she took control of the fighter direction once more. *Yorktown*'s radar took that moment to break down.

Lexington's Red section was in trouble with Zero fighters swarming around the planes as they tried to hit the Japanese bombers on their way home. *Yorktown*'s Orange leader wanted to come in, but could not get his flaps down. He came in very hot, a challenge to Lieutenant Campbell and his crew. But after a fight, anything could happen.

Yorktown's homing device was not working, so planes had to form up on *Lexington* and then be talked down by radio. Meanwhile the fighters were still engaging Japanese Zeros, some of them chasing the returning American bombers.

The hole in *Yorktown*'s flight deck had been repaired, and she was able to take planes. Although *Lexington* had been hit repeatedly by torpedoes, her flight deck was intact. So both carriers began landing their planes. Some planes were in critical condition, particularly the anti-submarine patrol from *Yorktown* that had been out four and a half hours.

The Japanese fighters going home stopped, just after noon, to take on the returning American strike force, and now the attention of the airmen focussed on trying to get in safely. The airwaves crackled with advice and questions and responses. *Lexington*'s Red and Blue fighter sections, getting low on gas, were orbiting the carriers, staying up there to protect the homecoming planes from any surprises by the Japanese.

The task force was still busy, but for the moment at least the tension was gone.

A Japanese torpedo bomber hit by carrier fire, flaming across the sky during the height of the Battle of the Coral Sea, May 8, 1942.

Among the U.S. naval commanders who played vital roles in the battle were Admirals Aubrey W. Fitch of the *Lexington*, Frank Jack Fletcher of the *Yorktown*, Frederick C. Sherman of the *Lexington* and Thomas C. Kinkaid.

The destroyer USS *Sims*, escort for the oiler *Neosho*, and the first to be hit by the fury of the Japanese attack. Despite her heroic fight against incredible odds she was finally sunk by enemy dive bombers. The carrier USS *Yorktown*, flagship and command center of the Coral Sea campaign.

USS *Neosho*, busily refuelling the *Yorktown,* just before the battle commenced. The *Neosho*, along with the *Sims,* would soon feel the brunt of the Japanese attack. Within days she would be totally incapacitated, a drifting hulk. The Japanese light carrier *Shoho* under attack by US torpedo planes. She is already afire from the combined efforts of planes from both the *Yorktown* and *Lexington.* Within thirty-two minutes from the first shot she was sinking in flames with more than 600 casualties.

The Japanese carrier *Shokaku,* undergoing the American air onslaught which utilized a simultaneous dive-bombing and torpedo attack. A Japanese torpedo bomber shown winging over one of the *Lexington*'s destroyer escorts at the height of the battle.

During a brief lull in the battle, men of the *Lexington* inspect severe damage done to the No. 2 gun gallery by Japanese dive bombers.

Aboard the carrier *Yorktown*, gun crews are at battle stations awaiting an aircraft attack from the Japanese carriers *Shokaku* and *Zuikaku*.

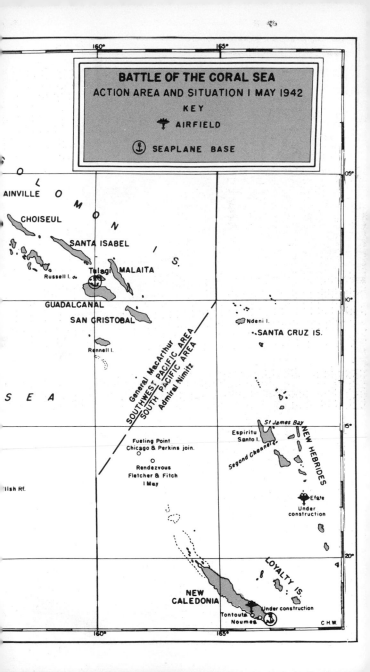

The *Lexington* is damaged by the mornings' attacks and her flight decks are littered with burning debris, hampering desperate attempts to keep the decks clear for her returning aircraft. Below deck the scene is one of exploding, fiery chaos.

By late afternoon the *Lexington* appears to be a doomed vessel. Another in the series of deadly explosions she suffered is shown here, its force tossing a plane from the flight deck.

Another view of the *Lexington*, totally engulfed in smoke and flame and listing badly.

A huge mushroom-shaped eruption marks one of the last fatal explosions that marked the end of the *Lexington's* chances for survival.

Captain Sherman gives the order to abandon ship and the men of the *Lexington* begin to gather on the flight deck preparatory to leaving the stricken carrier.

Men of the *Lexington* scramble down lifelines to safety as the burning, listing carrier continues to experience tremendous internal explosions.

The destroyers *Phelps, Morris, Hammann* and *Anderson* assist in removing the last of the *Lexington*'s 2700 crew men and officers. A great ship was about to die...

Chapter Twelve

The Fight from the Ships

From the vantage point of the cruisers and destroyers the battle took on a different aspect. The officers and men of these ships knew that the Japanese were out to get the carriers, although of course that did not mean a Japanese pilot would turn down a chance to sink a cruiser if he could. So it was the job of these support ships to fire and fire again, to protect the big flattops as much as they could from enemy planes.

When the Japanese torpedo planes were first sighted moving in on *Yorktown*, Captain Francis W. Scanland increased the speed of the cruiser *Astoria* to 30 knots, so he could conform to the movements of the carrier, and commenced firing the five-inch guns at long range. The gunners were using a 4.5-second fuse to put the barrage up over and beyond *Yorktown*. At 1115 *Astoria* claimed its first torpedo plane shot down on the port quarter by a direct hit. The plane faltered, and then disintegrated in flames.

A minute later *Astoria*'s gunners claimed another, a plane that had already dropped its torpedo, and came to within 400 yards of the cruiser's port quarter on the escape turn. There was no escape for this luckless pilot *Astoria* opened up with everything she had, and the plane plummeted into the sea, made one huge splash, and sank.

This minute—1116—was the longest of the day. One

torpedo bomber headed directly for *Yorktown* off *Astoria*'s port bow. The gunners were coming close, and the plane dropped prematurely, the torpedo running ahead of *Astoria*, and forcing one of the destroyers to turn hard to starboard to miss it. No sooner this, than another torpedo plane, its after fuselage aflame, tried to crash on *Astoria*. The plane came in on the port bow, made a gliding turn, very gracefully, and then splashed in the water 300 yards off the ship's side.

The action slowed down for the cruiser then—until the dive bombers headed in. Not all of them made for the carriers; *Astoria* was straddled by two bombs forward, and another pair aft, but they were not close enough to do any damage. The cruiser's gunners shot down one plane for sure, and believed they damaged another in this second attack.

When the action was over, Commander Chauncey Crutcher, the ship's executive officer, reported to the captain. There were several bomb or fragment hits.

One man had suffered a flash burn on the face from a nearby gun. Two ammunition handlers had dropped five inch shells on their toes: result, broken toes. But this was something to laugh about in the mess; they could all be thankful that the burning torpedo plane had not managed to crash the bridge, as had been the pilot's obvious intention. By three hundred yards *Astoria* was a very happy ship.

The cruiser *Portland* had an almost exactly similar experience that morning. Her small anti-aircraft guns claimed one Japanese torpedo bomber. She was off on the starboard side of *Yorktown* and was firing over her. From time to time she had to quit firing at planes approaching the carrier from the starboard bow—the Japanese came in so low that to fire at them was to endanger the carrier itself. But *Portland*'s consumption of ammunition in those few minutes of attack indicated the strength of the American barrage above the carriers. She fired 185 rounds of five-inch, 1399 rounds of 1.10-inch, and 2400 rounds of 20-millimeter shells. She had no casualties, but the barrel of one of the 1.10-inch guns ruptured from the heat. Luckily, no one was hurt.

During the bombing attack, two dive bombers tried for *Portland*, but were driven off by anti-aircraft fire. Four other planes came down strafing the cruiser, having dropped their bombs, or they may have carried small anti-personnel bombs, too. Commander W.B. Coleman, executive officer of the *Portland*, watched from his battle station:

> I noted about five splashes, from 100 to 200 yards, on both sides of the ship, which I believe were small bombs of 50 to 100 pounds. Two torpedo planes were sighted approaching the *Portland*, at low altitude, on our starboard bow. The rear plane was attacked by one fighter and was seen to zoom up to the right, and then appeared to fall into the sea. The fighter then attacked the leading enemy plane by diving and firing a burst, and then withdrew. The enemy plane appeared to be losing altitude and headed across the starboard bow of the *Russell*. The *Russell* shot this plane down. *Portland* could not fire at these planes because *Russell* was in the line of fire.

Coleman and Captain Benjamin Perlman were pleased with the performance of the crew, for *Portland* was a green ship. Most of the gunners on the small anti-aircraft guns were recruits, men with about five months' service. But they performed like veterans in this, their first battle. Each time a Japanese plane splashed in the water they raised a mighty cheer.

Cruiser *Chester* had a hairier time of it. Two torpedo planes, diverted from *Yorktown*, came in to attack the cruiser from the starboard; one was shot down by anti-aircraft fire before it released its torpedo but the second released the fish, and then was shot down to crash just off the starboard beam of the cruiser. The torpedo passed fifty yards astern, which was closer than Captain Thomas M. Shock liked to see them. And *Chester* had one casualty: Marine Pfc. T. J. Bianchi was wounded in the face and chest by fragments from a 20 mm. shell that blew up in a hot gun.

Lieutenant Commander Glenn R. Hartwig, skipper of the destroyer *Russell* described the action, when a whole group of ships were firing at twenty or thirty planes in a "melee." The confusion was so great that it was hard for anyone to tell precisely what was happening; the battle consisted of noise and smoke and the sight of things happening aboard carriers a mile and more away.

Because more than one ship were frequently firing at the same target, it is difficult to determine the effect of this ship's guns. Reports of the witnesses vary widely. These reports claim four planes shot down and one disappearing into distance leaving a trail of smoke. There is authoritative agreement on two of those reported shot down. The *Portland* indicated in a visual message of thanks that it observed one torpedo plane with its torpedo shot down by this ship. The other definite successful firing was also a direct 5″ hit at about 1000 yards, and although the shell passed through the plane without bursting, the plane broke up and dove into the sea. The destruction of the two planes listed as "possible" was witnessed by only a few observers so may have been the result of the *Portland*'s or the *Yorktown*'s fire.

The ships protecting *Lexington* had an even livelier time of it during the battle, The cruiser *Minneapolis* was in the direct line of approach of the dive bombers, standing off to the port of the *Lexington,* and as the Japanese planes concentrated on the carrier, they passed ahead, astern, and directly over the ship. Every gun was able to fire without worry about others, and they did. The men of *Minneapolis* claimed four planes, one on the port bow, hit by 1".1 guns and 20-millimeter on the starboard bow, hit by the five-inch guns, on the starboard quarter by the small guns, and one approaching from astern, shot down by one gunner, Gunner's Mate Third Class L.T. Van Wert. Captain Frank Lowry, commander of the *Minneapolis,* believed that two torpedoes were fired at the cruiser.

New Orleans, also protecting *Lexington,* had a hard time keeping up with the maneuvering of Captain Sherman, as he tried to dodge Japanese torpedoes. In the confusion, *New Orleans*'s gunners (as well as those of other ships began shooting at one plane that approached the ships, only to discover as it crash landed in the water, that it was an American dive bomber, not Japanese. But *New Orleans* was sinned against as well, Captain Howard H. Good reported that half a dozen five-inch shells very nearly hit his ship, and that one burst so near the starboard beam it severed the topping lift wire on the starboard crane.

Destroyer *Dewey* took much more of a beating. Early in the torpedo-plane attack, one of the Japanese planes dropped its fish and came in strafing, wounding six men on the port side by explosive bullets. Two near misses from small bombs fell very close, shaking the ship. Japanese fighters came in to strafe and one of them shot away the mainmast shroud. Gunfire from *Lexington* snapped the main radio antenna and put dents in the superstructure, but luckily hit no one. When it was all over at around 1130 the wounded were looked over again and a report made to the captain. A.S.N. Borich was seriously wounded by a bullet through the right cheek, and four other men were fairly seriously hurt by that strafing.

It was odd how *Dewey* was hit, for Destroyer *Phelps* which was also protecting *Lexington*, was not hit at all, nor was even the target of a Japanese attack.

The little ships performed very well, right to the end. When the Japanese had sheered off, around 1130, a single plane came in toward Destroyer *Morris*, and she opened up on it, along with *Lexington* and the other ships. The barrage was so thick in a few moments that the plane could not even be seen, then finally came the word from *Lexington* to the destroyer by TBS (talk between ships circuit) that the plane was a "friendly." It came in, limping, to try to land on *Lexington*'s flight deck, bounced, and slithered over the side. *Morris* then turned to rescue the pilot and his radio man, and hauled them aboard. Radioman third class C.H. Hamilton was no worse for wear, except for the ducking, but pilot Lieutenant F.R. McDonald, had been shot in the right shoulder by a machine gun bullet fired from a Zero fighter. He was taken below and turned over to Lieutenant (jg) N.J. Shultz, the destroyer's medical officer, who sewed him up and put his arm in a cast. He would survive to fight again.

Commander J.K.B. Ginder, skipper of the destroyer *Anderson*, was in the thick of it, and stood just off the 4000 yard mark from *Lexington*, where her guns could be of most help. Commander Ginder had one of the best views of all in the progress of the battle:

1116	During the attack the *Yorktown*, with her screen of destroyers and cruisers, opened out from the *Lexington*, about 15,000 yards.
1116.5	This ship opened fire on an enemy torpedo plane on the port beam, range 8000 yards, on a parallel course. Fired 45 rounds of 5″ ammunition in about 60 seconds. The plane was about 50 feet above the water. Once the plane appeared to be hit, when its left wing dipped considerably. The plane righted itself, however, on the same course, and then turned sharply to the left and went directly away from the ship. This plane had a torpedo and was trying to launch an attack on the *Lexington*. Bursts were close and the plane may have been damaged. No hits were observed.

During this attack the distance of this ship from *Lexington* varied from 2000 to 5000 yards. This variation was caused by the ship having to hold course to prevent masking the battery, having enemy planes under fire.

An enemy plane, 1000 feet overhead, fired machine guns at this ship, bullets striking the water in a line parallel to the ship from the bow to the stern, but about 150 feet out from the port side of the ship.

1117	Opened fire with 20 mm guns on three enemy torpedo planes on starboard beam, 1300 yards range, flying parallel but in opposite direction to this ship, 300 feet above the water. These planes were delivering a torpedo attack on the *Lexington*. No hits by our guns were observed on these planes.
1118	An enemy torpedo plane on the port bow was seen launching a torpedo, probably at a cruiser or this ship. The captain ordered "Hard Left Rudder." A torpedo wake was seen crossing the bow of this ship, close aboard. At this time both

the 20 mm and 5″ guns were firing at other enemy torpedo planes.

1119   The 20 mm guns opened fire on one enemy plane on the starboard bow, range 2500 yards, on a parallel but opposite course, headed in toward the *Lexington* to launch a torpedo. No hits on the plane were observed.

1120   Opened fire with the 5″ guns on one enemy torpedo plane on the port bow, range 7000 yards, on opposite course. About 60 rounds of 5″ ammunition were fired at this plane in about 90 seconds. Bursts appeared close by. No hits on the plane were observed. In about 45 seconds the plane made a sharp turn to the right, then returned to its original course and continued on. The *New Orleans* took up the fire on this plane. No hits on this plane were observed. The 20 mm guns fired a few rounds at this plane but stopped when it was seen that the range was too great.

Commander Ginder's report shows how elusive an attacking airplane can be; this one torpedo plane flew through the fleet, with hundreds of shells hurled at it, and yet the pilot managed to escape harm.

But not all of the Japanese that Commander Ginder saw that day were so lucky:

1121   Three enemy planes were seen crashing into the water near the *Lexington*. Splashes were noticed around the *Yorktown* in the distance. Heavy black smoke was seen pouring from the *Lexington*'s stack, while splashes were all around her.

The 20 mm guns fired at one enemy torpedo plane on the port beam, range 2300 yards, 300 feet above the water. The lead was insufficient, resulting in no hits on the plane. This plane had

134

delivered its attack on the *Lexington* and was retiring.

The 20 mm guns fired at one enemy torpedo plane, range 3000 yards. . . . no hits. . . . delivering a torpedo attack on *Lexington*.

1122 Changed speed to 33 knots. At this moment four or five dive bombers were seen diving on the *Lexington*. The *Lexington* went ahead of this ship at this moment.

1125 An enemy torpedo plane was seen to drop a torpedo near the *Lexington*. This torpedo apparently hit the *Lexington* as a large splash and flame arose from the *Lexington*'s side.

Three enemy dive bombers were seen diving on the *New Orleans*. Bomb splashes arose around that ship, about 1500 yards from this ship. The *New Orleans* did not appear to be hit. One of these planes was shot down by *New Orleans*' gun fire, and crashed into the sea close by. At this time, the sky overhead was filled with hundreds of bursts from A.A. fire from all the ships of this force.

1127.5 One of the *Lexington*'s planes landed on her deck. All ships continued to fire at several enemy planes flying low outside the formation.

1128 Passed through much fuel oil on the water. This oil evidently came from the *Lexington*. Observed a small yellow life raft (aviator's float) with a man waving a checkered flag at this ship. This ship was making 33 knots at the time and did not stop. It was later learned that this man was picked up by another ship. This, however, has not been verified.

No. 3 20-mm gun fired a few rounds at a low flying plane on the starboard bow. This plane had its wheels down but was quickly identified as

135

a friendly plane and fire was stopped. No hits were observed on this plane. One of the quickest means of identifying Japanese dive bombers is non-retractable landing gear carried on these planes. The plane then tried to land on the *Lexington*, during the engagement. It landed on deck, and fell over the side.

This last, of course, was Lieutenant McDonald and his radioman, coming in after being shot up, and by the time they tried to land on the carrier, the action was nearly over. *Anderson* cut speed to 25 knots at 1137, and settled down to the job of watchful waiting. Eight minutes later, her crew and the men of other surface ships watched, as *Lexington* began recovering planes. The sky was clear, the sun shining brightly still, and the Coral Sea looked just as peaceful as it had been on any other sunny day for the last thousand years.

Chapter Thirteen

"This Ship Has Been Torpedoed"

As the Japanese moved in, *Lexington* was better prepared for the battle than any other ship, for Captain Sherman had predicted early in the morning that the enemy air strike would come at about 1100. The prediction was quite in character for "Ted" Sherman; he was a brilliant officer and had progressed rapidly, for peacetime conditions, through the officer ranks, but he was also cocky, and sometimes brash. He would go on from this battle to become one of Nimitz's "fighting admirals," and he was already one of the principal advocates of increased air strength, although his own air training had not come until he was forty-four years old.

Aggressive and ebullient, he ran a taut and happy ship and had made *Lexington* into as good a fighting machine as the United States Navy had at hand in the spring of 1942.

From his bridge, the captain made sure that his ship was completely ready for attack. He had eleven fighters in the air for defense against bombers, and 14 SBDs for defense against torpedo planes, plus the *Yorktown* force. All anti-aircraft guns were manned and ready to fire, and the boilers were hot and prepared to give him 30 knots.

Captain Sherman was not totally happy with the conditions under which he would have to fight. The carrier being out in the bright sunlight was a definite disadvantage. Clear weather with unlimited visibility and no ceiling and no rain squalls gave him no place to hide, and for his liking the anti-torpedo plane patrol had strayed out too far from the ship. The planes were three miles out, flying at 2000 feet. The fighters, doing as they were told were at 10,000 feet. As it turned out, the Japanese came in above them, destroying the fighters' initiative, and then hedge-hopped right over the anti-torpedo planes at high speed before dropping down to attack.

As General Quarters sounded, Chaplain G. L. Markle was on the bridge, exploiting his privileged position as chaplain to get all the information he could about the fight that was coming. Although his battle station was below decks, he asked permission to remain on the bridge this day, and it was granted, on the condition that he find himself a steel helmet. There weren't any extra helmets up there—the officers and men were buckling them on as the fighter circuit reported the progress of the Japanese planes. Chaplain Markle went below, but everyone who owned a steel helmet was wearing it, and this was no time to get into ship's stores to secure an issue. Reluctantly he went to his battle station in the sick bay, and arrived just as the sailors were dogging down the water-tight doors, preparing for action.

Then, just before Captain Sherman's predicted hour of 1100, the loudspeaker in the sick bay began to crackle: Now hear this, now hear this . . . . . . enemy planes are approaching the ship . . . . . . they are twenty miles out . . .

From his observation point Lieutenant Williams, the supply officer who had volunteered to spot planes, watched as the TBD's went out to make contact with the incoming Japanese torpedo bombers. The rumor was floating through the ship that the Japanese numbered at least a hundred. He strained his eyes to see, but the haze was so great on the horizon that he could not see very much, just plumes of smoke as planes were shot down and smacked into the sea.

Then the squawk boxes began crackling again:

Here they come. . . .

Lieutenant J. F. Roach, junior medical officer of *Lexington,* was stationed in the engineer's battle dressing station, deep inside the ship, near the firerooms. All he knew about the progress of the battle was what he heard on the squawk box, and what he could sense and feel from this point deep inside the ship.

The *Lexington*'s bridge was stripped for action. The plate glass windows that protected the captain from the weather had been unlocked and slid down so they would not be broken and send flying glass across the bridge. This bridge on *Lexington* was located twenty-five feet above the flight deck, on the starboard side of the island, which rose above the deck. Since the flight deck was fifty feet above the water, the captain and the admiral had a fine view, the Admiral a little better than the captain, for his bridge was ten feet above the ship's signal bridge.

On the signal bridge this morning, the captain was accompanied by his key personnel. The navigator was Commander James R. Dudley, on duty in the wheelhouse. Also there was Commander Mort Seligman, the executive officer, and Commander Winthrop Terry, the communications officer. Commander Herbert Duckworth, the ship's air officer, was on the bridge, and so were a number of junior officers and enlisted men. They all looked very much alike, dressed in khakis and steel helmets. The only living thing on the bridge that morning that did not have a steel helmet as the battle neared was Wags, the captain's black cocker spaniel. He was "anchored" in the captain's sea cabin for the fight.

Captain Sherman watched speculatively as the Japanese came in at high speed, approaching his ship from the port side and heading in from starboard, too. They started high, and came down to 300 feet, some of them, before dropping. Others came much lower, just on the top of the water it seemed, to make their drops. Captain Sherman watched, and then reacted:

> I turned to port with full rudder to bring the first torpedoes ahead. From then on the torpedoes were coming from both starboard and port, and I maneuvered with full rudder both ways as I considered best to avoid torpedoes. Some from starboard crossed ahead, two others ran parallel to the ship, one on each side; some from port ran ahead; two ran under the ship without hitting. At 1120, first torpedo hit ship and exploded just forward of forward port forward gun gallery. . . .

Chicago *Tribune* War Correspondent Stanley Johnston was on the bridge of *Lexington* that morning, and he watched as the shimmering planes came diving in on the ship, fascinated by the sights and sounds of battle—and the smell: the reeking stench of cordite, blown up onto the bridge from dozens of guns.

Down below, in the engineers' battle dressing station, Lieutenant Roach felt that first torpedo as a rumbling explosion, accompanied by a violent shaking of the ship. Up in sick bay, Chaplain Markle was conscious of the booming of the five-inch guns and the crackling of the smaller weapons, and then came the shock.

From the boat pocket where he was spotting planes, Lieutenant Williams watched the torpedo planes come in:

A slick looking torpedo plane, the first time I guess we'd seen the big new torpedo plane the Japs had and they really roared in. One of them came in, I saw at least four streams of fire going for it and they seemed like they had him completely boxed, but he came right on in through it, and banked, dropped his fish, it was just sort of a little splash out there by the ship, about 600 yards, then came roaring right back in, pointed right at our battery and then he had the insolence to bank right about 20 feet in front of us—it looked like—and just sort of stood on end and roared up along the ship. Perhaps he was trying to distract fire from the ones that were coming in behind him. He did it, because our gunners, in spite of the fact that they shouldn't have fired on him after he dropped his torpedo, but should have gone after those still coming in—they couldn't resist the temptation and turned him over. Four or five streams of fire hit him. They turned him over as he was still in that bank, propped him on his back and by the time he got back to us again he was just a patch of gasoline, burning on the water beneath us.

We didn't have much time to worry about him though, for another one came right in behind him, caught fire about 200 yards out, and hit the ship right below Number 1 battery . . .

Commander Seligman's responsibility was the safety of the ship, and he began taking reports from damage-control parties, even as the torpedoes were hitting home.

141

That first torpedo shock was followed by a second, a minute later, which hit just about opposite the bridge. They had caused damage, but how much?

Commander Seligman called up Lieutenant Commander Healy, the ship's first lieutenant, who was in Central Station, and quickly learned that the torpedoes had caused some damage in Number 4 fireroom and flooding in Firerooms 2 and 6, but the situation was under control.

Not for long. Captain Sherman stood at the rail, watching and giving orders in a low, controlled tone of voice that did not even indicate he was excited, and he observed everything that happened:

In the meantime, dive bombers were making their attack from about a 70° angle. They were pushing over from high altitude, 17,000 feet, and were not visible until they were in the final stages of their dive. One bomb estimated at 1000 pounds hit the after end of the port forward gun gallery in the ready ammunition locker just outside the Admiral's cabin. Two other near misses hit close aboard aft on the port side and at first were mistaken for torpedo hits. Another bomb estimated 500 pounds, hit the gig boat pocket on the port side, and one 100 lb. bomb hit the stacks and exploded inside. There were one or more near misses aft on the starboard side, fragments killing and injuring a number of men in the stack machine guns, sky aft, and the after signal station. I personally saw a flaming bomb, approaching the ship from port, and burning with a reddish colored flame. I am unable to say whether or not it hit.

In sick bay, this spate of hits on *Lexington* was felt as "several heavy shocks which seemed to raise the ship up as if going over a hump." Then Chaplain Markle felt the ship roll from side to side.

142

I remarked to the senior surgeon that it sounded like a rough time above decks. He agreed and retorted with "It looks like this is the business."

Apparently, said Captain Sherman, there were seven explosions against the *Lexington*, two of them torpedoes, the rest bombs. Fires were started on the main deck near the "Admiral's country," beneath the incinerator, near the gig boat pocket, and in the forward marine compartment, on the starboard side near the forward elevator.

Chaplain Markle suddenly realized that he did not have his gas mask with him, and that was against regulations. He headed for his cabin, to retrieve it, making his way up three decks through smoke and darkness, and dust drifting through the passageway, coming from aft. He reached his cabin and fumbled around to find the mask, put it on his shoulder, and took a flashlight with him as he left the quarters. Then he hurried back amidships, and on the way to the sick bay:

I found four men nearly naked and crying for help, having been horribly burned. A Filipino cook who was there in the passageway helped me get the men on cots, take off the remainder of their clothes and give them a drink of water. One of these injured men was given a morphine injection to alleviate his suffering.

When the corpsmen arrived with the first-aid materials, we proceeded to care for the wounded, administering tannic acid jelly to the patients, who were largely cases with severe burns, covering large areas of the body. These men kept coming in from the 5-inch gun galleries on the port bow, some alone, other with help of a shipmate, many with clothes blown off and skin literally dripping from their bodies.

These men were survivors of the thousand-pound bomb that exploded just abaft Number 6 gun of the forward five-inch battery just after 1130. The hit was so nearly direct that it knocked the gun out, killed the complete crew of Number 6 and killed or wounded thirteen men on guns Number 2 and Number 4. Several other men were killed in the passageway on the main deck, and many others burned or hit by shrapnel. To add to the destruction, the bomb blast set off the preset five-inch ammunition in the ready locker in the cabin. The fire that started there swept through Admiral Fitch's cabin and the surrounding area.

Commander Seligman left the bridge just after this explosion and moved to the fire area to see how the repair party was functioning. There he discovered that Commander W.W. Gilmore of the supply service and Commander W.C. Trojakowski, the ship's dentist, had been killed in the passageway and that a number of men of the coding room had been killed or wounded by this bomb. He watched with approval as the damage control party fought the fire, using chemicals to put it out, quite disregarding the danger they ran from the five-inch ammunition exploding around them. Corpsmen led rescue parties up to find the living, without regard for the fire or explosions, and began moving them back toward sick bay.

He did not then know that in addition to Gilmore, the bomb blast had killed Lieutenant Robert Zwarsky, the ship's disbursing officer, and Junior Communications Officer Pat Jons, leaving only two men at the coding board, one of them seriously injured.

Lieutenant Williams, whose normal function was to relieve on the coding board, did not even know what had happened. He had his hands quite full there in the boat pocket, as the torpedoes from the planes shot down continued to run in. One struck directly underneath the gun platform.

It didn't throw us off our feet, was just sort of a big balloon and then a tremendous geyser of water and oil rose in the air. As we moved forward at about 30 knots, our gun platform stuck out over the side of the ship, and the water and oil settled down on us; we thought we were sinking. It was a solid wall of water and covered the whole battery with about a foot of oil and water. Before we had time to dig ourselves out from that somebody yelled "dive bombers."

Lieutenant Williams was so busy trying to follow the torpedo planes that he did not even see the dive bomber that dropped a bomb about 30 feet off his position, sending another geyser into the air.

I wasn't doing anything then but trying to keep from going crazy and turning and running. All the planes in the neighborhood were Jap. There wasn't any spotting to do. I was standing back of the guns without being in the way. Being an officer I had too much pride to go stick my head in the clipping room when a lot of the other boys had to be out there in the open.

He watched, fascinated, as another torpedo plane came zooming up, apparently bent on flying down his throat, and then another dive bomber, that came down and dropped its bomb. He saw the bomb skid along in the air, and somehow wriggle between the island and the stack, to go over the side without detonating.

The swiftness of it all, the noise and the shock took its toll, particularly of men who were not usually concerned with combat.

We had some mess attendants there who were supposed to be ammunition bearers but they had enough ammunition right there at the guns, so they didn't have anything to do. They were pretty well scared, back against the bulkhead. We broke into some quarters right near there, got some blankets, some brooms and tried to push the water and oil off to where it would drain out of the battery. The battery officer had plenty to do to keep the guns firing, directing the fire, so I had found plenty to do in getting the battery cleared up and there were an awful lot of shell cases to push out of the way.

One mess attendant, I remember I put a broom in his hand, he just stood there, he couldn't move. So I worked his arms a few times and got him going so he kept on going. I might add, too, that there was another one of these little mess attendants that was one of the finest boys I'd ever seen. He was scared plenty, too, like all of us, but I never saw anybody turn to and work better than he did.

Men reacted in many ways to the fright and bustle of battle. On the bridge, when that big black bomb whipped across on the stack side, Correspondent Stanley Johnston ducked automatically behind the bridge rail, just as did everyone else up there—at least those who saw it. Johnston's major reaction was one of annoyance. He was trying to dictate his impressions of the battle into a tape recorder, and make some notes at the same time, and the noise was so tremendous—guns firing, bombs blasting, torpedoes hitting, planes zooming by—that he could not hear any single sound, including that of his own voice. All that was around him was cacaphony.

What stuck in Lieutenant Williams's mind was the behavior of one man:

I'll never forget that little gunner on Number 3 gun, the battery. He looked like a dead-end kid himself. He was sort of lobe-eared, and had such bad teeth I don't see how he ever got into the Navy. To make matters even worse he had a head shave, which was sort of the vogue at the time among some of the sailors.

The thing I remember about that sailor was that when the dive bomber was coming in, his ammunition man standing right beside him had frozen stiff. Well, this little gunner was standing on one foot, firing, holding on to this 20 mm, firing up at the dive bomber, and kicking the hell out of his ammunition bearer with his other foot. He got results, too.

Down below decks at his action station, ship's doctor Roach saw nothing, and heard only explosions and racket above.

A few moments later smoke appeared through our ventilator shaft. We knew then, of course, that the ship had been hit, but we also knew that our fire rooms were functioning perfectly, as we could hear those burners turning up at full speed. We also could feel the motion of the ship through the water, so that we down below felt that all was well.

Chaplain Markle helped move men into the sick bay, and then helped move men from the sick bay onto the main deck. Then he hurried to the aviation dressing room, where more hurt men had been placed.

Although many were burned and wounded, they were all quite calm. They seemed to know me and appreciate a word of interest and assurance that we would stand by them. These were brave men bearing their

147

wounds and suffering in silence. As I spoke to some individuals, they were unable to reply, but would lift a hand to acknowledge my words of consolation and one or two said "Okay, Chaplain" which gave me assurance that my presence at the critical time was worth while.

After he had made sure that all was as secure as possible at the port five-inch gun stations, Commander Seligman learned that there was another fire in the starboard marine compartment. He hurried there, to find that it had already been put out, as had the one near the incinerator, and another in the gig pocket. That last had killed several men and wounded more.

Seligman got on the phone then to Lieutenant Commander Healy, and conferred about damage control. In spite of the hits so far, no dreadful damage had been discovered within the ship. Repair party people were inspecting and checking on the *Lexington*'s water-tight integrity, but there were no signs of trouble, and the gasoline system, that dangerous volatile combination of tanks and hoses, seemed quite secure.

Satisfied that Damage Control was doing a good job, Seligman went below to the dressing stations and sick bay, stopping here and there to talk to officers and men.

Down below, Lieutenant Roach and his men were suddenly assailed by an eerie silence. The action was over. There was nothing to hear, except the steady hum of the ship itself. They stood, uneasily, and waited. Then they felt the ship take a sudden lurch to port.

On the bridge, Captain Sherman felt her give, too, and checked quickly with damage control. The inclinometer showed a six degree list; Lieutenant Commander Healy reported that he was already taking action, shifting oil to correct the list. Main Control reported that all units were in commission. Firerooms Number 2, 4, and 6 were partly flooded, but the pumps were controlling the situation. The steering gear was in good shape and the ship was making 25 knots without any trouble. The one problem was that both elevators were out of commission. Both had jammed at the flight deck, where machinery had sprung or broken in the wells from the shocks of bombs and torpedoes. But that did not prevent *Lexington* from landing her planes, and bringing "the chickens" home was the next order of business. At 1130, Captain Sherman ordered the signal: "This ship has been *torpedoed*," to inform the task force of the turn of events. But he did not call for help, and the *Lexington*, from outward appearances was in good shape, although some of the pilots above noted that she was trailing a long oil slick.

Around 1200, Damage Control reported to the captain that the ship was on an even keel. The three fires had been extinguished, and the one remaining blaze, in Admiral's country, had been brought under control. Plane recovery operations were under way.

Yorktown landed her anti-torpedo plane patrol. *Lexington* landed her fighters and some of the scouts. Quickly they were refuelled and put back into the air, for no one knew if the Japanese planned another strike. Commander Brett's torpedo squadron headed for the ship, ten planes of the eleven that had made the attack on *Shokaku*. *Lexington* was ready to take them back aboard.

At 1220 Admiral Fitch sent a message to Admiral Fletcher to inform him of *Lexington*'s condition. Her maximum speed was 24 knots, Number 4 fireroom was still flooded and Numbers 2 and 6 were leaking. There had been many casualties, but all fires were out. Both flight-deck elevators were still jammed. This message was to give Admiral Fletcher the information, to consider as he pondered the next move of the task force.

Above and out around the sides of the Task Force, the fighters patrolled, noting the coming and going of planes, and Fighter Control kept them informed and soaked up their information:

1225 Red V Agnes: At least 2 aircraft bearing 315, distance 10 miles.

The force was still alert. Waiting, Fighter Control checked radar and radio, and in a few moments returned to the air:

1234 From Romeo: Aircraft 320 distance 19 miles. Friendly.

At 1236 one of the radar operators spotted a single blip on the screen:

Bogey 200 distance 17 miles:

Fighter Control was alert at once, calling:

Wildcat Red Leader: Vector 220 10 miles orbit. Remain on that. We have friendly planes coming in which may be attacked by Jap fighters.

Yorktown, too, was bringing home its birds. Just after 1230 the *Yorktown* attack group began landing. Lieutenant (jg) F.E. Moan brought his dive bomber down. The flaps failed, and Moan ran full tilt into the

150

islands, but the plane did not burn. He and his enlisted man, Seaman Second Class R. J. Hodgens had both been wounded. The landing crew got them out, and to sick bay for treatment. Then the deck men counted the bullet holes. There were twenty-two holes in the fuel tanks alone. The plane, courtesy of the Japanese and the crash, was a total loss, and was pushed over the side.

In addition to the talk between planes, talk from planes and talk between ships, the task force was receiving information from American and Australian ground-based airplanes, which were flying in the South Pacific that day. One plane reported a tanker and a freighter, which might or might not bring to the Japanese task force.

Yorktown, at 1237, intercepted a message from *Lexington* planes being attacked by fighters.

1238 Romeo:	Those are 10 SBDs, 3 fighters returning about 10 miles from ship.
Wildcat:	Your fishes are calling for help.

Lexington's planes were under fighter attack on the last leg of their long journey home. Lieutenant Commander Brett led his torpedo squadron in, and one nervous destroyer gunner began firing on the planes, but was stopped almost immediately. The ten planes landed, one by one. Then the patrol planes began to come in, and the pilots gathered around the carrier to swap excited stories of their experiences. Lieutenant Hall, one of the scout plane pilots, had engaged in a running dogfight with five Zeros just as he was shooting down a torpedo bomber. He had splashed two

Zeros, been shot himself in both feet, but had made it back to the carrier.

Ens. Leppla and his gunner, John Liska, were a part of the anti-torpedo patrol, and they were caught by another swarm of Zeros, fought their way out, and shot one down, then got a torpedo bomber. Leppla's forward guns were knocked out, and on the way back to the carrier they were intercepted by more Zeros, but Liska drove them off with the rear guns.

Ensign W.E. Wolke came back to talk of the Zero he had fought and the bomber he had shot down, and Ensign R.F. Neely claimed another two. Lieutenant Gayler, having shot down two Zeros in the fight above *Shokaku*, encountered a pair of the Japanese torpedo planes on their way back from the raid on Task Force 17 and shot both of them down. When he landed on *Lexington* he was the Navy's leading ace, with eight planes to his credit. Altogether the fliers of *Lexington* claimed some 28 victories or probables that day, at a cost of some 12 planes of their own.

At 1240, *Lexington* was still landing planes. Fighter Control asked Red Leader if he could find any bogeys, and he could not. *Lexington*'s fighters were coming in, very nearly out of gas, and *Yorktown*'s planes took the duty of combat air patrol.

From the bridge, Captain Sherman and Admiral Fitch were satisfied with results. It appeared certain they had sunk a Japanese carrier this morning, and the damage to *Lexington* did not seem great, that to *Yorktown* was not nearly so serious. Commander Healy assured the bridge that all compartments were holding and that progress was very satisfactory in damage control:

"We've got the torpedo damage temporarily shored up, the fires out and soon will have the ship back on an even keel. But I would suggest sir, that if you have to take any more torpedoes, you taken 'em on the starboard side."

It was a funny crack, and brought a smile on the bridge. The Captain could afford to smile. It seemed that everything was going to be all right.

Chapter Fourteen

The Ordeal of *Neosho*-II

During the long night of May 7, the men of *Neosho* and the handful of survivors of *Sims* waited hopefully for rescue. From the beginning of the Japanese air attack, before 11 o'clock that morning, the radiomen had sent out word that the Japanese were hitting the ship. Admiral Fletcher had received this word, the report that *Neosho* was being bombed by three planes in latitude 16°50′ South, longitude 159°8′ East. Then at 1600, the radio powered by the auxiliary had gotten off its message, that the oiler was sinking in latitude 16°38′ South, longitude 158°28′ East. That night, a dispatch from Pearl Harbor told Fletcher that *Sims* had also been sunk, so the Admiral took the steps that Captain Phillips expected. He dispatched the destroyer *Monaghan* to speed to this area and search for survivors. By all rights, *Monaghan* would have found the *Neosho* in the morning; the sky was clear, the weather fine. But when morning came, *Neosho* was still drifting, still very much alone.

As dawn came, the miserable men in the boats drew near the hulk of the ship. She was sitting very low in the water, with a list of almost thirty degrees. Every man aboard could tell that she was settling. The process was slow. The leaks had not burst wide open, but the process was continual. If it went on

154

much longer, the tanker must go down. The starboard side of the main deck was now under water.

The captain looked around him, at the taut, gray faces. Every man was covered with fuel oil, the leaks and the dousings of the night had made sure of that. Fuel oil was over everything. The deck was slippery with it, the rigging dripped water and oil, and the stink of it was in every sailor's nostrils.

As the sun came up, so did the wind. The captain could tell it was going to be another choppy day, fine for a ship at sea, with a force-five wind, but not at all fine for survivors riding a wreck. He looked at the sun, and at the men around him, and he waited. Officers and men counted the minutes and then the hours, praying for rescue.

That morning, the men were still confident that rescue was on its way. It would naturally take a little time for the ships sent out to find them, for the planes to get off on their searches and circle the area where they had gone down, then move out to allow for the *Neosho*'s drift.

Captain Phillips took stock. About him he had loyalty. Lieutenant Commander Firth, his executive officer, was critically burned on the face, hands, and left arm, but he continued to offer the captain any service he could perform. Unfortunately, in his condition there was not much he could do. But for that matter, except for a few precautionary measures, there was not that much anyone could do.

Most of the exec's responsibility now devolved upon Lieutenant Commander Brown, the navigator. He was resourceful and above all cheerful, and there was much to be said for that in these trying hours. Lieutenant Verbrugge, the engineering officer, was also unfailingly cheerful. Like the others, he was covered with fuel oil, his hair matted and his clothes filthy. Yet he went down, time and again, into the slippery engineering spaces, to see if there was anything he could do to improve their situation. As of this morning he had found nothing.

Pharmacists Hoag and Ward had spent the night trying to comfort the burned and the wounded. They had practically no medical equipment, and the condition of the deck was miserable—slanted, and filthy with oil and human contamination.

This morning, as Captain Phillips called the boats to come in to the ship, Hoag and Ward checked the condition of their charges. Sadly, then, they had to report to the captain that CM 2c Leon Brooks had died during the night from his wounds. When Chief Dicken brought *Sims's* leaky boat up against the hulk of *Neosho* and the tanker men awkwardly tied her up, he reported that Chief Yeoman Clark of the destroyer had also died during the night. The bodies were brought on deck, the captain conducted a little service, and the two sailors were dropped over the side, their weighted corpses sinking swiftly into the deep blue water. No one even knew Chief Clark's first name or initials, for all his friends had gone down with *Sims* already.

The burial party ended, Captain Phillips tried to remove the sombre thoughts it had engendered by putting the men to some hard work. All the injured were brought on deck, off the boats; all the extra people, whose weight was threatening the stability of the overladen craft. Hoag and Ward reported that in addition to Commander Firth, twenty three men were badly injured or burned. Some of the seamen were assigned to help the corpsmen keep the sick as comfortable as possible. The captain organized a water supply group. This detail was to check out water tanks, and draw water, without contaminating the supply. From every available compartment, the men found receptacles, and filled them. Then they brought them up to deck and put them down carefully on the port side. No one knew what was going to happen to *Neosho*. They had to be prepared. Another party did the same with food, and when they came back the captain announced the rules. Fresh water would be used for drinking only; there was no excess available for washing.

It was a blow. Everyone was grimy with oil and dirt. Seawater simply rolled off it in beads, leaving a sticky mess. If a man had a bar of soap, it still did not take the viscous oil away.

The injured were in particularly bad shape, for they had been unable to protect themselves during the night and the oil slopping on the decks had permeated their clothes. Captain Phillips sent men down to rummage through the cabins, and to break out clean clothes from the small stores for those whose clothing was totally saturated. The party found blankets, and these were brought on deck and changed for the filthy blankets of the wounded.

When the food and water details had finished their job, Captain Phillips assembled the stores amidships on the port side of the ship, and gave orders to begin stocking the boats. It might be necessary at almost any time to abandon the sinking hulk, and he was making what preparations he could.

The two *Neosho* boats in the water would certainly not accommodate all these men. *Sims*'s boat was leaking worse than ever. The mattress that covered the hole stove in her side was totally soaked, and the leak let water come in around it. The boat was brought alongside, and a party patched up the hole as best they could with wood and canvas. From the deck the men cast doubtful eyes on the repairs; in case of trouble no one wanted to brave the seas for long in that boat.

But three boats for sixteen officers and ninety-three men of *Neosho* and the fourteen remaining survivors of *Sims?* That meant forty-one men in a boat, and every survivor on the hulk of *Neosho* knew their chances thus of making land were almost not worth talking about.

The captain knew, too, and he put his officers to work on the problem. Several parties began stripping wood, to construct life rafts to replace those seven life rafts that had been cast off.

Somewhere out in the Coral Sea, four officers and 154 men were floating, waiting for rescue, not knowing that no one in Task Force 17 had the slightest understanding of their situation.

Lieutenant Verbrugge moved around the deck, looking from time to time at the two motor launches still aboard the ship. They were big, heavy boats, and the ship's designer had never considered their launching without the power of the ship behind them. The launch and one other boat on the starboard side might as well be given up. The starboard deck was under water, and the sea was breaking over the boats. Even had it been flat calm, the task would have been impossible. But the port motor launch was another matter. Lieutenant Verbrugge began considering problems of math and physics that he had not worried over for a long time. By the beginning of the day watch, much of this work was accomplished. The men settled down then to wait, through the heat of the day, for the rescue that would surely come.

They had no idea that Admiral Fletcher had found

Takagi's carriers, and that the Japanese had found the Americans, or that a major battle was in progress that morning, a few hundred miles to the north of them. They waited.

Chapter Fifteen

The Explosion

Aboard *Yorktown*, Admiral Fletcher was assembling information about the Japanese and their possible intentions. He was wondering whether to stage another air strike, or to send the Attack Group of cruisers and destroyers in to make a surface attack on the Japanese forces. Fletcher's information indicated that *Yorktown*'s planes had made six hits with thousand-pound bombs on one carrier, and put three torpedoes into her. They had left the carrier on fire forward, and obviously very badly damaged. *Lexington*'s air group had apparently hit another carrier, this one of the *Shokaku* class, and they said they had put three one-thousand pound bombs into her, and five torpedoes.

Thus, if both enemy carriers were out of action, and one of them probably was sunk, it would indicate that a surface attack could be launched without much fear of Japanese air power. A surface fight was very much in Fletcher's mind, because he was one of the old school of naval officers, trained in surface-ship warfare.

More intelligence came in, and Fletcher kept pondering. There was time, for Captain Buckmaster still had to repair the boilers of *Yorktown*, and *Lexington* obviously had some damage that had to be given attention.

Some two hundred miles away, Admiral Takagi was making the same kind of estimates. With the discovery of the American force early in the morning, and the launching of the air attack Admiral Takagi had called for more help. His Sixth Cruiser Division, consisting of six ships, was refuelling from the oiler *Iro* that morning, 100 miles southwest of the Shortland Islands. That division stopped the hoses and began steaming toward Takagi, to help him if possible in a surface engagement.

The returning Japanese planes reported they had struck a carrier of the *Saratoga* class and had hit her with nine torpedoes and ten bombs. They had also a *Yorktown* class carrier with three torpedoes and eight bombs. Both those carriers, said the Japanese pilots with great emphasis, were *definitely sunk*. Besides, the air strike group had scored several torpedo hits on a battleship.

From Takagi's point of view, then, the battle had been an absolute success. He knew that *Shokaku* was hurt, and had dispatched her homeward, after taking on the serviceable planes she had to offer.

Captain Mineo Yamaoka, senior staff officer of the Fifth Carrier division, told Admiral Hara how pleased he was with what they had accomplished. The Japanese had been waiting for years to test their carrier ability against that of the Americans. Pearl Harbor had proved nothing; the carriers had not been in home waters, much to the disappointment of the Japanese carrier men. The American air resistance had been almost laughable back in December. But this day they had fought the Americans in the first big carrier battle of the war—in history for that matter. And the Japanese knew they had won. Whatever damage had been wrought on *Shokaku* was as nothing compared to the sinking of those two carriers. The real value of the carrier force was proved beyond doubt, and this was realization of Captain Yamaoka's most cherished dream.

Admiral Hara agreed, and so did Admiral Takagi. They made no effort to confirm the claims of the carrier pilots. One reason for this failure was the difficulties in which the land-based air forces found themselves. The Twenty-Fifth Air Flotilla had been given a primary responsibility to carry out reconaissance, but it also had the job of softening up and watching the Port Moresby area, in anticipation of the landings there. On paper Admiral Yamada, the commander, had about a hundred planes for the job. In fact, he had been suffering severely from a shortage of parts, replacement planes, and some losses. On the day before this battle the *Goshuu Maru* had delivered a dozen fighters to Rabaul, but even so the Fourth Air Group was having difficulty in putting together a single attack unit. Much of the fighter strength was being used for attacks on Port Moresby.

It would have been desirable for the land-based air planes to join the carrier craft on the attack against the American task force, but 25th Air Flotilla did not have the planes in the right places. A large proportion of the fighters had been transferred to Lae to hit Port Moresby. Several of the big patrol boats had been shot down, and there were not enough observation planes to give Admiral Takagi any real information about the enemy, particularly after the battle. Takagi's air intelligence, then, was far inferior to that of the Americans, for as he was considering the battle in light of the carrier pilots' reports, Admiral Fitch, on *Lexington* was getting reports from other allied aircraft that indicated the Japanese were still in fighting trim. He learned of one unhurt carrier that had been spotted by a main land plane. That carrier obviously was *Zuikaku*. Fitch did not know so much, but at least he knew that the Japanese had one undamaged carrier, he thought one had been sunk, and he was unsure about the condition of a third.

Admiral Takagi saw no point in hanging around this area. He had won the battle, and had nothing to fear from American air. His concern was that his planes had been badly shot up. Thirty had been lost in the fighting, and some thirty pilots had also been lost. There were no carrier planes available closer than Truk. What hurt him, and what hurt Admiral Hara particularly, was that the loss of *Shokaku* and the shortage of planes would keep Fifth Carrier Division from steaming to join the forces that were going to attack Midway, lure the American fleet out of Pearl Harbor, and put an end to American naval power in the Pacific.

Admiral Fletcher and Admiral Fitch continued to mull over their situation, too. They were waiting for the return of all aircraft, and it would be another two hours or so before they would know that every plane that was coming back would have made it. Until then, they must concentrate on landing, rearmament and repair.

Aboard *Lexington*, Commander Ault's dive bombers, for the most part, were home. Ault was not yet back. The torpedo planes were back, and when it was all sorted out, Captain Sherman gave credit to five men for making hits on the Japanese carrier. They were Ensign N.A. Sterrie, Ensign T.B. Bash, Ensign H.R. Mazza, Lieutenant E.W. Hurst, and Chief Air Pilot B.C. Shearon. The captain was satisfied that the carrier was sunk.

He was still chuckling over Commander Pop Healy's advice to take further torpedoes on the starboard side, when with a frightening roar, an explosion

163

shook the ship. From the bridge it seemed to come from amidships, down deep in the bowels of the carrier, but no one knew what it was. The best guess up there was that a 1000-pound bomb had failed to explode on impact, and had now somehow jarred loose and blown up.

The explosion came at 1247. Commander Seligman did not even know what time it was, he had been so busy checking into the condition of the ship. He was just entering the hatch leading to the sick bay forward, when the force of the blast, aft and below him, blew him through the scuttle. He was dazed for a moment, but unhurt. He picked himself up and hurried aft to try to find out what had happened.

He saw a fire blazing in the passageway of the Chief Petty Officers' quarters, and around the office area nearby. It was especially hot and bright near the gunnery office. But this kind of fire, on the second deck, was not regarded as too dangerous. It did not affect the life of the ship.

Damage control was having its problems. The forward fire hoses did not have any pressure, the mains had been broken somewhere along the line. While repair parties tried to find out where the trouble was, others brought hoses from aft, and began playing them on the fire on the second deck. Commander Seligman tried to reach the bridge. He could talk to Captain Sherman, and he reported what he had found. But when he tried to get Central Station, he could not. He began to gather that something more serious than seemed apparent had happened down below.

At his action station in the engineering dressing station, Lieutenant Roach heard the explosion, and felt it shake the ship. In a moment the telephone was ringing, calling his party to the hangar deck, with the report that there were many wounded men there. Roach and a corpsman left the station, and went forward trying to reach the hangar deck. They found that several compartments had been hit, and that the burst had caused them to flood with oil and water. It took them long minutes to discover this, then to retrace their steps and take the long way around. When they reached the hangar deck, it was in semi-darkness, and the area was full of smoke. Roach asked what had happened. No one knew for sure, but there seemed to be a fire down in main control. The repair parties were beginning to fan out.

Lieutenant H.E. Williamson was standing just outside the door to Central Control when the blast came. The concussion hurled him against the guard rail, which broke. He fell against the switchboard. The explosion was followed by a rush of air, which came through the doorway like a hurricane, and pinned him up against the switchboard. It was not clean sea air, but a wind of sparks and streaks of flame, followed by gray and black smoke that dashed after the fires. The fires came, cherry red and blazing white, and destroyed the oxygen—until Lieutenant Williamson was choking in the smoke. He could not breathe, but he held his breath and buried his face in his clothes.

From around him he heard screams and cries, and he shouted out to the others to hold their breaths and not panic, and they would get out of there.

The lights were still on by some miracle, but it was not much help—the smoke was so dense he could not see the lamps. He led a party out through the scuttle onto the hangar deck and began calling for help. Men scurried from every corner and began pulling the injured and the choking men out of the scuttle.

Men were staggering up onto the hangar deck from

main control, alone, or supported by their buddies. Some of those Lieutenant Roach examined were dead. Some were severely hurt—burned, or cut and bleeding—victims of explosion. For the most part it seemed to be burns, but the obnoxious gases had complicated the injuries.

Lieutenant Roach set to work to help. It was hard going, for the whole hangar deck was bathed in acrid smoke. With the lights out, depending on emergency lighting, he could scarcely see what he was doing. He could not work at all without a gas mask, and that made things harder. He moved to the forward end, where it seemed a little lighter, and set up his emergency station there.

Lieutenant Williams and the 20-millimeter battery with which he was working this day had moved away from their action stations. They were still on alert, but the battery was secured because the smoke from fire-fighting below kept blowing up through a ventilator that opened right on the battery. So the whole unit took to a perch on some steps alongside the ladder that led up the ship's side to the flight deck. When the explosions came, Williams's first thought was for his safe and his office. As a paymaster he had control of huge amounts of money. Zwarsky had $210,000 in his safe, which Williams had turned over to him a few hours earlier. Williams had over $100,000 in his own safe.

Williams hoped that he might make it down to his office near main control, but he was quickly disabused. Another explosion shook the ship, and the fires down there broke out anew.

Down below, Lieutenant Williamson went back into the scuttle to help bring out men still in there. Then came another blast, and he could tell that it had come from the machine shop. Smoke and flames came

166

spurting out onto the deck. Williamson turned, found the chief engineer, and reported that the gas fumes must be going off throughout the ship.

Lieutenant Frederick W. Hawes led one party down into the lower deck to try to rescue men, and Ensign Rockwell led another. They brought eleven men out of that area, most of them fainting from smoke inhalation. Hawes was overcome, but dragged himself back to the hanger deck, got a little breath and went in again. He was overcome a second time, but did the same.

The men were hauled through the scuttle, and then the sailors of the hangar deck brought dollies that were usually used to handle planes. The wounded and vomiting were loaded on them and moved to the far end of the hangar deck where Lieutenant Roach was supervising the aid teams.

The blast tore steel doors as though they were match covers, every one of them from central control, forward on that deck through the Chief Petty Officers' mess, the junior officers' mess, and to the main sick bay, three hundred feet away. Surgeon White was standing in sickbay, when the blast threw him through a door, onto the deck. He fractured his ankle and wrenched his shoulder. But he dragged himself to his feet, and said not one word about his own injuries, but began tending the men as they came in.

Smoke began pouring into the sick bay, so dense that Dr. White had to get the men out. He moved his patients, and they took over the captain's quarters amidships. Captain Sherman had no need of the space then, he was on the bridge, trying to save his ship.

Commander Seligman at first believed the fires were local, and the explosion confined, but soon he realized that the blast had come from below the armored deck, and that these fires up above were not the main trouble. Yet they were a big problem.

The ship's service phones went out. A bad fire broke out from the main deck down to the area of Central Station, just forward of the main elevator. All pressure was lost in the fire mains forward. Rudder indicators to the bridge went out, although at the moment steering control was still working. By using emergency techniques, steering control was retained on the bridge, but how long that could last was questionable. The forward gyro-compass system was not working.

The second explosion was accompanied by heat, smoke and gas so strong that men with ordinary gas masks could not enter the area to fight the fire. Only rescue breathers were useful. And the supply of these was limited, as was that of oxygen bottles. Soon Commander Seligman and the fire-fighters could find no more of them. Yet somehow, officers and men of the repair parties kept on going down to fight that fire in Central Station, using only ordinary gas masks. As the danger to the ship became apparent, they were joined by men of the air department and deck divisions, who were not assigned to these jobs at all, but wanted to help.

The fire spread up through CPO country, and soon reached a compartment where five-inch ammunition was stored. This went off—more explosions, more fires—and the fire fighters were hampered by the danger of shrapnel, and the increase in carbon monoxide that sent them staggering through the smoke after a few moments in the heat.

It would be days before the captain and Seligman would really be sure of what had happened. Right now they were still thinking in terms of a delayed

Japanese bomb. But what had really happened was this:

One of those Japanese torpedoes, which had struck the port side of the ship, and had not seemed to do too much damage, had actually ruptured a number of the fresh-water tanks, and the gasoline tanks located inboard of them. The torpedo had created a mining effect—it had bulged the plates of the ship inward, and damaged the inboard bulkhead. Behind this bulkhead in the vicinity of Frame 63, where the torpedo had struck, was the motor-generator room and gas-control room. Very slowly, for nearly two hours, gasoline vapor had seeped out of the bulging tanks, and built up into a concentration. The motor generators continued to run.

Men had checked the compartment but had found nothing amiss. The room had been filled with carbon dioxide as a precautionary measure during the attack, but once it ended, the carbon dioxide was not renewed, and the gasoline vapor sank down low, while the testing was going on high in the compartment. So, in essence, the generator room was a huge bomb, just waiting for the proper concentration and a spark, to explode. The spark came at 1247.

The detonation blew flames and vapor through the gas vent pipes which led into CPO country, and started those fires that began the explosion of the five-inch ammunition. It demolished the generator room, and badly damaged Central Station, and the compartments nearby. It severed all communications to Central Station, and cut off the fire mains forward.

If the men could have used those forward firehoses, the flames on the second deck might have been controlled. But they could not.

Lieutenant Commander O'Donnell, the gunnery officer, somehow brought up two hoses from aft, and they were led into the scuttles of the five-inch ammunition hoists to starboard, One hose was led into the dumb waiter of the food distribution room for the CPO mess, trying to flood CPO country, where the fires blazed. The hoses had good pressure, and the fire fighters began to hope.

Lieutenant (jg) R. O. Dietzer, the V-1 division officer, was in charge of the gasoline system. He made sure that the gas system on the starboard side was functioning properly. It was. He also secured the whole system on the port side, as a protective measure, and ordered that the gas-control room on the port side be flooded with water and smothered with carbon dioxide. Every gallon of gas had been emptied from this system by this time.

Commander Seligman realized that the fires in the CPO area were very serious, and the water shortage was not helping any. But two hours after that first explosion, he also felt that the men were making headway, and he was feeling very woozy from smoke inhalation. He decided he could take a break for a moment and go on up the flight deck for some air.

Correspondent Stanley Johnston was in the navigating cabin. Earlier, after the attack had ended, he had gone to look for his typewriter in "Admiral's country" where his cabin was located. He had found his cabin and the Admiral's in shambles, soaked with fire-extinguisher chemicals, and the first still burning. Five-inch ammunition had been stored here, and some of it had exploded. But much of the rest was scattered about the whole deck, and the projectiles had been forced loose from the cases by the fire and heat. When that happened, the projectiles fell out of the brass cases, and the fire got into the powder, making a sizzling flame that reminded him of the old "sizzlers" boys used to make by breaking a fire cracker in two and lighting it at the middle. Johnston went to look for Duke, the admiral's cabin boy, whose action station was in the pantry. He found him there, dead from the first blast, near the accordion he played when the ship went into battle.

Johnston had then gone to the navigator's compartment to try to write up his notes and get a story ready to send back to the Chicago *Tribune*. He was sitting there, along with Chief Quartermaster Solomon, who was writing the ship's log. Then came the big explosion.

Johnston hurried below to see what had happened. He went to the wardroom, found it vacant, and then to the junior officers' mess, three decks down. There he saw fire, and since he did not have a mask, he had to scurry back up topside before he was overcome.

Soon he learned that Pop Healy had been killed, seconds after he made that wisecrack to the captain about torpedoes. Now, nearly four hours after the battle, more men were dying than had been killed by the Japanese attack.

Johnston moved around, talking to people who were taking a break, trying to get the picture of the explosion for his story.

On the bridge, the captain had his problems. He was able to use speaking tubes to communicate with engineering, and two other departments, but for the rest, he had to communicate by sending messengers. An hour after the first blast, fires had burned through the main electric cables, and the steering was lost. The captain was able to use the "trick wheel," located down in the steering room; he gave orders which were transmitted through a speaking tube, to a quartermaster down below in his blind position. But then the fires burned out the speaking tube, and the bridge was cut off from steering entirely. Captain Sherman was not going to be defeated this easily. He took a page from the sailors of the past, and ran a line of men from trick wheel to bridge—spread along four hundred and fifty feet of deck, four decks down. The bridge gave the orders, and the word was passed, from man to man until it reached the quartermaster at the bottom.

After the second great explosion, Surgeon White and his patients were driven out of the captain's quarters by smoke, and they moved to the forward flight deck, the most smoke-free place on the ship. This was the end of the line.

Down below on the hangar deck, Lieutenant Roach saw that the forward end of the deck was totally untenable, and the rescue parties brought the men aft. The men were treated, made ready for movement here, and then evacuated up to the flight deck. With the new series of explosions, Roach was told to evacuate the hangar deck and move up himself. He could see fires burning cherry red at the forward end of the deck, so he knew the moment had come. He could see virtually nothing else, even with a powerful flashlight. Vision was limited to two feet in front of him. Getting those wounded up on the flight deck was going to be a massive job. But Roach and Lieutenant Hirsch, and some twenty-five corpsmen and volunteers did get the wounded out, one by one and two by two, and to safety up above. Then Lieutenant Roach went on deck himself, leaving behind a hangar deck where the whole forward end was a mass of flame.

Commander Seligman had just reached the flight deck, and was standing on the forward elevator, when a second explosion of great strength shook the whole ship. It came from the starboard, just forward of the elevator well. The elevator was jammed up, but down through the cracks at the edges he could see sheets of flame.

He shouted for a hose, and someone brought one from aft, and played it on the top of the elevator. It seemed to slow down the fire in the well.

Back down into the smoke of the hangar deck, Commander Seligman gave a rush of orders. Carpenter Nowak hurried off to make sure that all hangar-deck sprinklers were turned on, and Lieutenant Commander O'Donnell went to see that all the torpedo heads stored on the mezzanine were sprinkled down to protect them from the heat.

By this time, the medical party evacuated, the hangar deck was very hot. The fire was spreading slowly aft. Every few moments there would be another explosion near the elevator well, and while the well itself seemed to be cooling, from the water pouring down off the flight deck, still the fires moved aft.

All this time, the Air Department of the ship was going about its work, landing planes. One of the combat air patrol planes developed troubles. The propeller was stuck in low pitch, which gave tremendous vibration at high speed and cut down the maneuverability of the plane seriously. The pilot radioed *Lexington*, which was ready to take him on, but before could happen the pilot managed to get control of the prop.

Yorktown was rearming her planes. Her Number 7 and number 8 boilers were repaired by 1300. She had 40 dead, 26 seriously injured, 40 wounded, and one missing in action. But she was ready to fight again if need be.

At 1315 Admiral Fletcher suggested that the force retire in view of enemy fighter plane superiority and the fact that an undamaged carrier had now been reported. Admiral Fitch concurred. Still the planes were coming in, and both carriers were waiting to account for all of them, sadly to declare them missing before they moved.

Lexington picked up Ensign Jorgensen and Radio Man Burnetti, who had been wounded. *Phelps* picked up *Yorktown* fighter pilot, Lieutenant (jg) Richard G. Crommelin, who had made a forced landing in the middle of the fleet. And still the planes came in, slowly.

Admiral Fletcher now made his plans, He might rearm *Yorktown* next day with *Lexington* planes and renew the attack, he said. That seemed doubtful, more talk for the record than actuality. If the Japanese had fighter-plane superiority at the moment, and another undamaged carrier, those facts were not going to change any. Fletcher was ready and itching to move out, to head south southwest at best practicable speed.

Yorktown reported at 1335 that she was prepared to make maximum speed. All her damage that affected the engineering department had been repaired.

Fitch demurred. He was heading up north to close the returning planes and pick them up, rather than steam in the opposite direction just then.

Fletcher put on the pressure:

CTF to CTG 17.5:   *Yorktown* reports all planes returned or hope given up.

The implication was clear enough; Fletcher was in a hurry to get out of there.

Three minutes later Fletcher was on the air again:

CRF 17 to CTG 17.5:   When do you propose to head to the southward?

Fitch was obdurate:

As soon as aircraft recovered.

But now, Captain Sherman had to admit the sad truth that he had been hoping would change. He had reported earlier that the fires were out on *Lexington*, and at the time they had been. But he had not yet reported the explosion of 1247, considering that he could control this damage. With the fate of the task force depending on *Lexington's* maneuverability, however, by this time Captain Sherman could not long delay telling Fletcher that he had troubles. He indicated that the fires were not out. In a message a few minutes later Admiral Fitch indicated that the *Lexington* could still make 25 knots, as she was.

But then the steering problem became really acute. The chain of men functioned as well as they could, but the result was not precisely immediate reaction from captain to quartermaster, since it travelled across several hundred men. Thus the strange antics of *Lexington* were very noticeable. With the continued troubles, just at about the time the men came up from the hangar deck, Lexington turned fighter director control over to *Yorktown*. *Lexington's* radar had failed.

Up above the carriers, the drama of the pilots was being played out. One dive bomber could not find the carrier and the fighter director talked him into circling and climbing to try to get a better view. Then he flew a course of 100 degrees for five minutes, and *Lexington* asked *Yorktown* to try to pick him up on the screen.

All this while, below, the informational messages were passing back and forth. Admiral Fitch advised

Fletcher that he had strong indications still another carrier had joined up with the Japanese. Fletcher had reports from Pearl Harbor, relayed from shore-based air, that indicated one enemy carrier was badly damaged and the second was undamaged.

The missing dive bomber managed to make contact, and found its way home. The other dive bombers were back now. Eight of them came in fast, heading directly for *Lexington*, not answering recognition signals because they were so nearly out of gas they had no time to waste. For a moment, the force was alert, and one destroyer did open up on the group of planes, but very quickly they were recognized and the situation understood. They began landing, even as the explosions grew in intensity below the decks of the *Lexington*.

Two planes were still out there, and the drama continued. They were Commander Bill Ault, the leader of the dive bomber squadron, and of the whole air group, and 5V53, one of his pilots. Now, the radio log told a swift shorthand story that hinted at the action and the emotions of hundreds of men in ships and planes, as they tried to save a burning carrier and bring home two eagles.

Yorktown:	We have 5V53 at 100. 7500. Do you want him to climb?
Lexington:	to *Lexington* Plane 5V53. We do not have you in sight.
	(*Lexington* had been trying to locate this lost plane and Commander *Lexington* Air Group (CLAG) by radar.)

176

| 5V53 to *Lexington:* | We are going to try to make the nearest land. Advise please. |
| *Lexington* to *Yorktown:* | Please relay important radio messages. Our coding room temporarily out of commission. |

There was an understatement if there ever was one. *Lexington*'s coding room had been blown to smithereens by a bomb in the battle. Now she was making do, but not with coding. It was essential, of course, that if a direction be sent to 5V53 about land, that the Japanese not know precisely where the American plane would be heading, so the message must be coded. *Yorktown* would have to do it.

| *Yorktown* to *Lexington:* | 5V53 is asking you if you'll let him go to the nearest land. We can't get him on the screen. |
| *Lexington:* | Roger. |

Now came more of the nuts and bolts of warfare. Admiral Fletcher was getting ready for the next day. *Yorktown* reported seven fighters ready to go, plus another that would be ready next morning, and one on *Lexington.* Then there were 11 dive bombers and six more that would be ready the next day. She was missing six dive bombers and their pilots. She had eight torpedo planes.

Fletcher announced at 1442 that he was considering a night surface attack. He checked the force; would the ships have enough fuel for this, also assuming that they would have to move at high speed the next day, and could not fuel from the cruisers until the day after? The question was particularly directed at the destroyers, those foxes of the sea, which burned huge amounts of fuel in comparison to their capacity, when they moved in at high speed to deliver a torpedo attack.

Up above, 5V53 was still waiting for the word, and somewhere out there Bill Ault, CLAG, was trying to get home.

Then came a break in the silence.

| CLAG to *Lexington:* | I am steady on course 110. Acknowledge. |

Lexington was rolling with the punches of the explosions. She could not help. She could not even answer; if there was to be any assistance it would have to come from *Yorktown.*

Yorktown to *Lexington:*	Your 5V53 is asking for instructions.
Lexington:	We can't help him. Did you get last message?
Yorktown:	Acknowledged.

Then *Lexington's* worst explosion yet struck just at the elevator, and the flames began burning red below.

On the air, 5V53, flying somewhere away from the carrier search for land, could reach Bill Ault, and was talking to him.

| 5V53 to CLAG: | Bill, I received. Your strength 2. So I think you are a long way off. If you reported two hits we would like to be given credit for one hit. |

The carriers could hear this transmission, but they could not find the planes. *Yorktown* searched, but CLAG was not on her screen. Neither was 5V53.

Ault now called *Lexington*.   Can you hear me and do you have me on the screen? I have gas left for about 20 minutes.

Yorktown to CLAG: I can hear you. You are not on screen.

Ault made one last desperate try.

CLAG to *Yorktown*:   Shall I circle? Do you want me to gain or lose altitude? I have gas left for about 20 minutes.

Yorktown: You are not on the screen. Try to make the nearest land.

It was a death sentence. *Yorktown* did not know where CLAG was. CLAG did not know where he was. The possibility of finding land was remote, and everyone concerned was aware of it But there was nothing to be done. Up there, CLAG flew along, watching the fuel indicator drop, moment after moment, not knowing what he was going to do, hoping that either the carrier would suddenly appear over the horizon, or that the dim outline of land would come up. Wounded, his radio man wounded, and alone, Commander Bill Ault faced almost certain death in that moment. He knew it; he faced it with real heroism.

CLAG to *Yorktown*:   Nearest land is over 200 miles away. We would never make it.

Yorktown to CLAG:	You are on your own. Good luck.
CLAG to *Yorktown:*	Please relay to *Lexington.* We got one 1000-pound bomb hit on a flattop. We have both reported 2 or 3 times. Enemy fighters. Am changing course to North. Let me know if you pick me up.
Yorktown to CLAG:	Roger. You are on your own. I will relay your message. Good luck.
CLAG to *Yorktown:*	OK. So long, people. We got a 1000-pound hit on the flattop.

And that was Bill Ault's valedictory. From that moment on, turning to avoid fighters, he was too busy to call again, or his transmissions were unheard—or he had gone down.

There was no time on *Lexington* or *Yorktown* for any sadness or reminiscence about Bill Ault. For just at that moment, 1456, Captain Sherman made a signal to the Task Force, hoisting a flag.

This ship needs help.

With that second series of explosions, Captain Sherman and Commander Seligman knew that their chances of saving the ship were not now so very good. The forward part of the carrier was ablaze, both above and below the armored deck. But the terrible and decisive factor was that the damage-control parties had absolutely no means left to fight the fire that was spreading aft on the hangar deck. It was just a matter of time until the fire reached the two dozen torpedo warheads on the mezzanine.

Aboard *Yorktown* Admiral Fletcher could see that the situation of *Lexington* was growing worse. He ordered the rest of the task force to open out the formation around *Lexington*, and stay away from her, so there would be no danger of collision.

Damage-control parties were trying to get the steering back to the bridge. An electrician's mate volunteered to be lowered down into the leg of one of the tripod masts—a hollow tube about two feet in diameter—where the wires were strung. He hoped to be able to repair them.

A sling was rigged by others, and an emergency telephone hooked up. Then he went down. The line went out fast, but then came a gasping cry. The heat from the fires burning all around the tube had made it so hot he could not stand it. They pulled him up just before he collapsed.

The interior of the ship was now in total darkness and the light came from bull's-eye lanterns. But any light was almost useless in the smoke down below. That second series of explosions shook the whole carrier, and down on the engineering decks, it wrecked the ventilators. The engineers and firemen began to choke. Usually the temperature down there was about 100 degrees. It jumped to a hundred and fifty.

Admiral Fletcher sent a hurried message to General MacArthur's headquarters, announcing the serious nature of *Lexington*'s damage and asking for land-based air cover. Captain Sherman asked the navigator the course and distance to the nearest land. Perhaps he could beach the ship and still save her. He asked the distance to the closest point in Australia. The navigator came up with the figures, and Chief Quartermaster Solomon set to work plotting the course.

Up on the flight deck, Commander Seligman ordered Ensign Dowling to loosen all the ship's life rafts, and be prepared to distribute them fore and aft. For the first time he was thinking about that dreadful possibility of abandoning ship.

There was only one phone working on the whole ship at this point, just before three o'clock in the afternoon. It was the telephone to the main control, or what was left of it. Even this line was scratchy and it seemed certain that it would go out any moment. So Commander Seligman sent a messenger down to the Chief Engineer, advising him that it might be necessary in a short while to abandon ship. He then ordered all unoccupied personnel to move to the starboard side of the ship, fore and aft, for *Lexington* had begun to list again, seven degrees to port.

Seligman made his way to the bridge as quickly as he could move. He conferred with Captain Sherman, told him what he had seen and what he had done. He also recommended that the engineering plant be secured, before all means of escape of the men below was cut off by the fires. Captain Sherman listened, and ordered all the men up on the flight deck.

It was the end, wrote Correspondent Johnston in his notebook.

Meanwhile, Admiral Fletcher had asked Captain Sherman by Talk between Ships what assistance the fleet could give *Lexington*. Fletcher also wanted to know if the carrier could still launch and land planes, and how many fighters she could launch.

Plane 5V53 was still in the air, with a little gas left—wherever she might be. *Yorktown* called, but the plane did not answer. Time was running out.

Lexington now asked *Yorktown* to land the fourteen planes *Lex* still had circling in the air. Then she called the other ships to stand by in case it was necessary to abandon ship.

There was one bright spot: *Lexington*'s plane 5V53

radioed *Yorktown* at 1536. "We have made it."—the pilot and radioman had been able to find land.

But that was the only good news of the hour. Captain Sherman was still trying to save the ship, but the chances were now almost remote. At 1600 the one remaining phone was so weak he could scarcely hear Main Control. The forward bulkheads were so hot the paint was peeling off in large blisters. All personnel were shifted aft, and at 1630 engineering spaces were totally abandoned, the safety valves were opened and the ship lost all power. She was dead in the water.

That was the ultimate decision. When the engineering spaces were abandoned, the last of the water power was cut off. Captain Sherman hoped that destroyers could come alongside and fight the fires from outside, and he asked Admiral Fitch to bring the little ships up. Fitch issued the order, and then told Captain Sherman to disembark the wounded from the flight deck and all excess personnel onto the destroyers when they came alongside. The end was very near.

Chapter Sixteen

The Ordeal of *Neosho*-III

Destroyer *Monaghan* had steamed out on the evening of May 7 to try to find the wreck of *Neosho* and save the crew if they could not save the ship. But on the morning of May 8 they came to the reported position of the tanker, and found nothing at all. Then, in a search of the vicinity they still found nothing at all. And meanwhile, the men of *Neosho* waited in the sun.

Captain Phillips noted with dismay the increasing water in the lower compartments of the ship, and the constant drag of the list to starboard. He sent a crew to throw overboard everything on the starboard side to reduce the list. A party tried to break the starboard anchor chain on deck. They wedged it and they hammered it and they tried to twist it, but it was no good. That chain had been meant to withstand torque and pressure, and it was doing so. They could have burned it with an acetylene torch, but they had no power and no torch. So they ran it out with a rush, hoping it would tear itself loose and sent the anchor down. No such luck—the bitter end held. Instead of eliminating the weight on the starboard side, as they had hoped, they had increased the drag.

Engineer Verbrugge now went below again, hoping without any real reason that something would have changed so that he might be able to raise steam. He checked the engine room and the fire spaces, and came to the conclusion he knew he would reach. There was nothing any human being could do to get *Neosho* going again.

While he and his party were below, Verbrugge also checked every corner of the spaces, to make sure there were no wounded, or even dead, lying down there below. He found none. Then he rechecked the bomb damage to the cargo tanks. There was no change.

Back on deck, Verbrugge kept looking at the motor launches. These were the last hope of the men of *Neosho*. If he could get at least one of them over the side, perhaps they could save themselves, if worse came to worst and no one found them. For as the day wore on, and neither plane nor ship appeared, captain and crew began to wonder what had happened to Task Force 17. It was conceivable that the force had been destroyed in a battle. The captain would have liked to take a navigation fix, but it was rough and none could be considered reliable. The captain sent a message, in the clear, and not repeated very many times, via the portable transmitter. They had to conserve fuel. He noted their position and their condition.

That afternoon, as they all waited, Captain Phillips idly replotted the last given position taken by the navigator before they were wrecked. Suddenly he started. The position was wrong! The navigator had taken a fix on the sun and on Venus, and had plotted it at 16°25′ South, 157°31′ East. As the captain replotted the observations, he found that their actual position at about the time of the action was 16°09′ South, and 158°03′ East. It made a difference of many, many miles as a point on which to start looking for them.

185

Suddenly it seemed very chill. If they had given a wrong position, and were not now heard, then there was small chance that they would ever be found. It was no good chewing out the navigator; he was inexperienced and careless, but it would not help to argue with him. The captain sent the message of the real last position. As the shadows of late afternoon lengthened, the officers of *Neosho* who knew the facts were feeling very low. It was going to be a long night.

Chapter Seventeen

Abandon Ship!

The destroyer *Morris* was the first ship to come alongside *Lexington* in response to Captain Sherman's call for firehoses. Captain Gilbert Hoover, commander of Destroyer Squadron Two, already had her standing by, not far out from the stricken carrier, so she was only 1200 yards off the port quarter. The explosion, the black smoke, and the slowing of the big ship told the story. Speed fell to 10 knots, and then she came to a halt, as *Morris* moved up. She came up alongside the starboard side.

After Captain Sherman had made the semaphore signal for help—his lights and all else in the communications section broken down, Admiral Fitch had ordered him to remove the wounded from the ship as well. So as *Morris* came up, the men on deck were putting the *Lexington*'s casualties into life boats, to move them over to the destroyer.

Morris moved too far forward. She could have backed down, but by this time the *Lexington* lifeboats were in the water aft, and so she had to pull away to prevent being fouled by the carrier's overhang and five inch gun mounts. The wind was on the starboard bow, which did not help anything.

It was half an hour later, then, 1635, before *Morris* had come alongside about amidships and was pumping water. Two 1½-inch hoses were rigged aft and one forward and a 2½-inch hose was hooked up to the fire and bilge pump in the engineroom.

The destroyer *Anderson* also closed up on *Lexington* and circled her waiting for orders from higher authority to help. At 1609 came the message from *Lexington* that she had lost all control, and had abandoned the stations below deck. *Anderson* and *Hammann* circled *Lexington,* clockwise. The boat launched by *Lexington,* filled with wounded men, was in the water and in the way. Captain Hoover ordered *Hammann* to pick up the boat, so *Morris* could exert full efforts at fire-fighting.

A few minutes later *Lexington* launched another boat. But *Hammann* had still not picked up the first one, and Captain Hoover told the captain to speed it up.

Then, before *Hammann* could comply, came another order, to come alongside *Lexington* and pass fire hoses. *Anderson* had the same order at the same time.

The two destroyers had to maneuver carefully in these close quarters—*Hammann* passing behind *Anderson.* Now *Anderson*'s orders were changed—she was to stand by to come along side *Morris* and take off some of the *Lexington* people, who were being passed to that ship.

Destroyer *Anderson* was ordered to go to the port side of *Lexington* and fight the fire. But the wind was brisk, and *Lex*'s list was very decided—almost 30 degrees at this point. *Anderson* moved up, along the port quarter of this windward side of the ship, and could not fend off. She bumped her starboard bow against *Lexington.* Luckily no damage was done, and she backed away, to try again. But in spite of the skill of her captain, the ship could not stay alongside the

188

carrier without being smashed, and *Anderson* had to head off for the port bow and stand there.

Hammann was getting ready to rescue survivors, for it seeemed certain now that *Lexington* would be abandoned. Commander Arnold E. True told his exec., Lieutenant Ralph Elden, to get nets over the side and fenders out. All lines were made ready for rescue efforts. Ensign Holton was assigned to take the ship's whale boat, and Ensign Krepski was put in charge of the gig.

The three destroyers were then formally assigned to stand by *Lexington*, while Admiral Fletcher tried to make up his mind whether or not he would stage a night attack against the Japanese force.

While *Morris* was playing hoses on the fires, men not needed on *Lexington* were climbing down lines to reach her decks. Commander Seligman was moving aft on the flight deck, where he had ordered the ship's company assembled except for those fighting the fires. He gathered officers around them and told them to keep an orderly evacuation into the boats.

Correspondent Stanley Johnston, his story forgotten for the moment, was doing his best to help get the wounded away from the ship. He went into a flame-filled compartment, and pulled one man who was injured and blinded out to safety. He went back in for others. He came up on the flight deck with a armload of life jackets and distributed them to men waiting to be rescued. He was invited to leave the ship among the first but refused. He would stick around awhile, he said.

The flight deck was quiet and orderly. The airmen had taken Mae West jackets and pneumatic life rafts from the planes, and lines were rigged down the sides of the ship. The men of *Lexington* were ready to abandon if they had to.

Besides the destroyers, the cruisers *Minneapolis* and *New Orleans* were standing by to help. *Minneapolis* had orders from Rear Admiral Thomas C. Kinkaid to be prepared to take on 1200 survivors if necessary. She moved over to a point 2000 yards off the *Lexington*. The busy *Hammann* and *Anderson* had been unable to stop long enough, in the face of constant orders, to pick up those two boatloads of *Lexington* wounded, so they moved to *Minneapolis* and she took them aboard. *New Orleans* then circled around and took station a hundred yards off the port bow of the carrier, facing in the opposite direction.

Aboard *Lexington*, Captain Sherman had finally realized that the fires were out of control. Explosions were coming rapidly now, as ammunition and gas pockets went off. The warheads on the hangar deck were reported to be at 140° by the last man to leave that inferno. (He burned his hand touching one.) Ready bombs were stored not far away, and Captain Sherman now worried lest the ship blow up at any moment.

On deck, Commander Seligman was even bringing out mattresses to serve as additional flotation gear for the ship's people.

Lieutenant Williams, the paymaster, was suddenly stricken with a sense of responsibility and disaster. What about those hundreds of thousands of dollars in the ship's safes, for which he was responsible? Although the forward elevator had been lifted a foot in the air by the explosions, Williams got a running start and leaped over, and made his way up to the bridge. He wanted to tell the captain that he couldn't get the money out.

Captain Sherman, however, had a few other things on his mind. Williams was stopped by the officer of the deck, who patted him firmly on the shoulder and turned him around to go back to the flight deck. That money was not going to be spent by anyone, any time, anywhere.

Lieutenant Williams did gather up all the papers he could find including the pay records of the men for whom he was responsible. Then, like the others, he waited.

Admiral Fitch and Captain Sherman were conferring, keeping up with the condition of their deteriorating ship. Then, at 1707 Admiral Fitch called down from his bridge:

"Well, Ted, let's get the men off."

That was the order to abandon ship. Captain Sherman made it formal, and the disembarkation they all dreaded began. Sailors began throwing rafts overboard. The marines took off their shoes and left them in a neat line on the flight deck and then began climbing down the long ropes that led fifty feet to the sea.

Besides the other destroyers circling or lying alongside, destroyer *Dewey* now came up over the horizon, having failed to find the airman reported in the water that had sent her off on search. Admiral Kinkaid ordered her to close on Lexington and see if she was needed to rescue men. *Phelps* was also ordered alongside, and the two ships took position about 1000 yards to windward of the burning carrier, and sent their boats to pick men out of the water.

Hammann steamed close to *Lexington*. Ensign Holton in the whale boat and Ensign Krepski in the gig cleared the ship and began looking for survivors in the water.

Having lost way, *Lexington* was drifting broadside to starboard, and soon many men were strung out in the water upwind of her. The ship's two boats, then, were directed to concentrate on rescuing men who did not seem to be in a position to be rescued by a destroyer. The boats ferried back and forth rapidly, and the men came aboard on both sides of the destroyer, clambering up the cargo nets, ladders and bowlines that had been strung out.

After getting the wounded off, Lieutenant Roach and the corpsmen swung down the lines from the side of the carrier, into the water. Many men, unaccustomed to rope work, burned their hands severely as they slid down.

In the water, they found it hard to swim away from the ship. Lieutenant Roach tried several times to swim away from the side, and got exactly nowhere. At first he thought it was suction, about which he had heard a good deal. Then he realized that the ship was drifting down faster than he could swim. He began swimming alongside the *Lexington*, and made some progress. He swam to the bow, and then could move out 150 yards away from the ship. A boat from *Minneapolis* came along and picked him up. As he was pulled into the boat, Lieutenant Roach realized that he was completely exhausted. Well, there was reason enough for it. They had been at action stations since dawn, and then fighting the fires after the Japanese left. There had been nothing to eat all day long, and nothing to drink since the water pressure failed.

Lieutenant Roach was lucky. One of his corpsmen was not so lucky. This sailor was standing on a raft alongside the *Lexington* when another explosion shook the ship. When *Lexington* was made ready for war, steel plates had been welded over the portholes, to prevent anyone from breaking blackout regulations. This explosion tore loose one of those plates, and sent it spinning through the air with the force of a projectile. It struck the corpsman in the head and he died instantly.

About twenty minutes after the order to abandon

ship was first called out, *Hammann* backed off and moved alongside *Lexington*'s starboard beam. This was a very ticklish time, for *Lexington* was pushing downwind, and there was grave danger that some men would be crushed between the sides of the two ships. But *Hammann*'s captain True had used foresight—a big fender had been put over to port, and it kept the ship from actually coming up against the side of the carrier at the water line.

Morris was having problems with the unpredictable carrier even before the final act began. Survivors continued to pour down onto her decks, and the injured were taken to the wardroom, where they were treated by Lieutenant (jg) Herbert J. Schulz, the ship's doctor. The uninjured were coming down the lines. Then, an explosion just below the hangar deck blew an eight-inch hole in the side of the carrier, just opposite the hatch on *Morris* that led to the Chief Petty Officers' quarters. Four minutes later came another explosion that was just opposite the bridge of the destroyer. The hot blasts shook the little ship.

Eight minutes after the order to abandon ship was passed, *Morris* was moving away to make way for *Hammann*, for *Morris*'s decks were completely filled with men from the carrier.

It was not easy. There were three hundred men in the water between the stern of the destroyer and the stern of the carrier. Life rafts bobbed up and down. The whaleboat of the cruiser *Minneapolis* came by the stern with some forty survivors in it, heading back for the mother ship.

Captain H.B. Jarrett of *Morris* very gingerly began to back away. He backed the port propeller three times, in spurts of ten seconds each, and then they got out of the way of the hulking *Lexington*. As the destroyer slid from the side of the carrier, and the gap widened aft, the hundreds of men who lined the rails and crowded the decks of the *Morris* set up a cheer, and the men still aboard *Lexington* responded. They were giving their last words of encouragement to the ship and its captain.

Morris's stern moved around out of the immediate area of the swimmers. She backed both propellers at two-thirds speed. It was the proper maneuver to be sure they did not drag any men under or grind them up, but it was not fast enough to clear *Lexington* properly. *Lexington* came down on the ship, and her overhand carried away a piece of the after windscreen. One of the five-inch gun mounts scraped a searchlight and smashed it, and then carried away a stay to the foremast.

Morris continued to back until she was clear. Then she moved to the side of *Minneapolis* and transferred her survivors to the cruiser—2 injured men and two hundred uninjured.

In the wardroom, as *Morris* moved, Lieutenant Schulz was treating the wounded. One man was dying. He had been burned over a third of his body—third-degree burns with charred flesh and bones protruding, and his face was nearly gone. The other wounded were hurt by burning powder and some shrapnel from the exploding ammunition. Two men had suffered "shell shock" and sat staring without seeing anything at all.

The transfer to *Minneapolis* was not easy. She was standing about 100 yards off the starboard quarter of Lexington. The seas were growing heavier in late afternoon, and the destroyer took quite a pounding. Her port side was dented by the cruiser's fenders, and one opened a seam in Number 2 fireroom some six inches long. The port whaleboat davits kept fouling the splinter protection of the amidships guns, so *Morris* got clear, and was then ordered to move toward *Yorktown* and screen her, so that another destroyer of the screen could come in and pick up more survivors. There were still more than 400 *Lexington* survivors on the *Morris*.

She also had aboard Wags, the captain's dog. An ensign had gone into the captain's cabin, searched through the smoke, and rescued Wags, wrapped him up in a life jacket, and handed him to Private Smith, the captain's marine orderly, who lowered him down onto the destroyer before she pulled away.

Destroyer *Anderson* stood off the port bow of *Lexington* to pick up survivors. She was about 800 yards from the carrier and men were swimming to her, or coming in life rafts or boats. Captain Ginder ordered the port boat, the gig, into the water. Machinist's Mate First Class Ernest Morris was the boat engineer. Coxswain Leonard Pipitone was the coxswain, and Seaman Second Class James M. Marron was the bowman.

Coxswain Pipitone steered the boat astern of *Anderson* and began picking up men in the water. Soon there were thirty men in the boat, and she was very low in the water. She was taking water all the time, and more as the damp cargo was dragged over the side. *Morris* ran the bilge pump and everyone who was able bailed, with the three buckets available. Still the water was up eight inches over the floor boards. But they made it, without swamping, back to the port quarter of *Anderson*, and unloaded the survivors, who clambered up the cargo nets and ropes.

The boat went back, to the bow of the *Lexington* this time. No one was there. Coxswain Pipitone then steered down the port side. They took in tow one life raft with one marine aboard, and then picked five men out of the water. The heavy seas were now breaking over the sides, and the boat was shipping water, even though everyone bailed, it seemed to be gaining.

Pipitone then steered over to a heavy laden life raft. They counted noses: forty men aboard—too many to bring into the gig. So *Morris* tried to take it in tow, but the two-inch line fouled around the propeller and the shaft. Seaman Marron then went overboard and cut away the line, but the boat was drifting—down on the destroyer *Dewey*. The destroyermen threw two lines out as the life rafts came down the port side, and took off the men of *Lexington*. The gig drifted down the port side, and from the bridge came a hail.

"What's the matter.?"

"Line fouled around the propeller."

The captain of *Dewey*, Lieutenant Commander C.F. Chillingworth, Jr., then ordered them to come alongside so the boat could be hoisted and the line cleared. But then he changed his mind. As the boat came alongside, he ordered the crew to abandon, and the boat was abandoned. Enlisted men did not argue with officers. *Dewey* then took over the boat, and sent it out under one of its officers to take on more *Lexington* personnel. When the men had been rescued, the *Dewey* officer put the boat in gear and opened the throttle. He jumped out and let the boat go, while the crew, standing along the rail, wondered just what kind of war this was going to be.

Anderson's second boat, the motor whaleboat, was sent out at 1726. Her crew consisted of Seaman Third Class James B. Anderson, the signalman; Machinist's Mate Second Class George Masten, the engineer; Seaman First Class James Carlyle, the coxswain, and Seaman First Class Philip Watkins, the bowman.

As the boat was lowered, it swung in toward the

ship and struck a 12-inch ball fender. This impact cracked two boards amidships, below the gunwale. The boat set out for *Lexington* anyhow, leaking. As the men began picking up survivors it took water all the time. The boat was then loaded with thirty men, and also took in tow a life raft with another ten aboard. All the men who could bail were bailing and the bilge pump was going full blast. Along came another ship's boat, empty except for the crew, and the *Anderson* boat turned over the life raft to this whale boat.

The crew then headed back to their own ship, the *Anderson*, but with the heavy load and the leaking, they made for the nearest ship, the *Dewey*. The coxswain moved alongside, the survivors were put aboard the destroyer, and then engineer Masten tried to start the engine again. There was 18 inches of water in the bottom of the boat and the engine was obviously water-soaked. It would not start. Captain Chillingworth ordered the crew to abandon the boat and they did, and it was cut loose.

Aboard the *Lexington* the explosions seemed to come almost constantly. An hour after the order to abandon ship was given, there were still a number of officers and men on the flight deck. There was absolutely no panic. In fact the debarking had an almost unreal, leisurely air about it. Men would go to the side, look over, and decide they would wait until the crowd thinned out. Correspondent Johnston walked around the deck as if he were taking a stroll. He found the after five-inch crews still at their guns, waiting until the last in case of a Japanese air attack. Now, as the end came, they began throwing five-inch ammunition into the sea, so it would not explode and endanger the men still aboard the ship.

The men on the decks of the carrier were almost

unbelievably calm. Someone had brought up a dozen gallon cans of ice cream from the ship's service canteen, and men sat under the wings of planes, shoveling it in, using paper cups and wooden spoons. Lieutenant Gayler dived off the fifty-foot deck into the water, swam out about 100 yards, and then swam back, climbed one of the ropes and reappeared, waiting for the others of his squadron to decide to get off. It was too lonely down there to stay, he said. Lieutenant Williams gathered up all his pay books and wandered to where a group of men were lounging among the planes. Lieutenant Commander Weldon Hamilton had assembled them there, gathering around him the fliers, mechanics and others of his Bombing Two squadron. To keep their minds off problems any might think they had, he was giving them a pep talk on squadron unity. Then, it was time to go. Hamilton led his men to the edge of the flight deck, and they began climbing down the ropes onto the deck of the destroyer below.

"Here," said Lieutenant Williams. "Catch these pay records. You want your pay records, don't you?"

"Hell yes," said Skipper Hamilton. "Toss 'em down."

He looked up at Williams. "Then come on down yourself. We want the disbursing paymaster with us."

"All right."

"Sure. Come on, now."

So Lieutenant Williams slid down the line to the destroyer and soon felt her cool deck beneath his feet. It was a pleasant change from *Lexington* where the deck had been growing so hot he could feel it through his shoes.

Commander Seligman sent junior officers to check every space that could be checked, to be sure there were no dead or wounded, to bring out any living men and make sure they got off the ship. He checked on his checkers. Many men and officers did not want to leave the ship and had to be ordered over the side.

Most of the men were off the *Lexington* by 1800. Admiral Fitch and Captain Sherman were the last to leave the bridge. The captain had stepped down several times to make inspections forward but this time he did not go back. Admiral Fitch went forward and down to be picked up by the destroyer *Anderson*. Captain Sherman made one final trip aft to see that all were off. He found several men aft on the starboard side of the ship and in the port after gun gallery. They could see men in the water below, having trouble getting away from the ship because of the drift. There were twenty or twenty-five men in the water or on life rafts, and the destroyers and their boats had gotten them.

Destroyer *Hammann* had been lying alongside for some time, and Captain Elden had tried to explain to the men that they must cast off the lines from *Lexington* and push out. *Hammann* then came up on the port quarter and shot over a twenty-one-thread manila line with loops in the end. Commander Seligman snared it, leaned over the cargo nets and dropped the line in the middle of the rafts. He saw a man reach out and pick it up and then he went forward on the port side to look for stragglers.

He saw Captain Sherman approaching Lieutenant Hawes and several others at the after gun mount and speaking to them. They had refused to abandon ship until given a direct order. Now they had that order.

All the men were then off except Commander Seligman and Captain Sherman. Seligman saw Lieutenant Commander Paul Ramsey sitting in a small boat astern, and he waved to him, hoping Ramsey would spot him and pick him up, and the captain too. But Captain Sherman was determined to be the last man to leave his ship, without question, so he ordered Seligman off, and the commander slid down a line and dropped ten feet into the water, where Ramsey picked him up.

As he went down the line, a tremendous explosion rocked the *Lexington* and sheets of flame surged out of the starboard side, above and below the after 1.1 gun mount. Debris flew through the air, scattering like shrapnel in all directions.

The captain had one more mission. He picked his way back to the island area, and found his cabin. He went in, found his best cap with the real gold braid on it, and put it on his head. He never knew, there being a war on, when he would be able to get any more real gold braid. Then he went back to the flight deck and looked over.

Captain Sherman saw Seligman swimming below, as the explosion continued to rack the ship. He looked around, double-checking what he already knew, that no living person was left aboard the ship. Then he swung over the side and down a line, hand over hand, until he dropped into the water. He was picked up by a whale boat from the USS *Minneapolis*, hoisted by the collar and the seat of his pants, and dumped into the bottom of the boat.

The cruisers *New Orleans* and *Minneapolis* were preparing to take on most of the 2700 officers and men coming off the carrier. *New Orleans* was standing to windward of the *Lexington*, on the port beam, and so many men who dropped into the water were brought close aboard the ship and had only to clamber up the cargo nets. The ship had out fifty lines with bowlines, to haul them aboard. Captain Good had considered putting *New Orleans*'s bow alongside *Lexington* but was worried by the fires—when he came up the whole between-decks was ablaze and flames shot out over the water. Soon he was glad he had not, as that last great explosion wracked the ship and would have wrecked at least some part of the cruiser and caused many casualties among the men clustered on her decks.

Boats were out chasing the rafts and men drifting to windward, so they would not slip away, and the rafts coming to leeward simply moved up against the side of the ship. The men of *New Orleans* also unlimbered throwing guns, and fired lines across the rafts, then hauled them in.

From the *New Orleans*, Captain Good had a bird's-eye view of that last great explosion abaft the amidships area. He thought a magazine had gone up, for the entire center of the flight deck blew out, and almost all the rest of the deck was aflame. Some of those men on rafts were still hanging onto lines on the stern, and *New Orleans* sent boats, which rescued them all. Captain Good then made a survey, and discovered no more men in the water. One of the destroyers searched out to windward and found none, either.

The whaleboats of *Minneapolis* were working as hard as any, and in the constant banging and pushing against the sides of the ships, they were both stove and finally had to be abandoned. The crew of one boat was picked up by *New Orleans*. The crew of the other managed to transfer to the *Minneapolis* motor launch before the boat sank—except the engineer, who went down with his boat, but was saved by the *Hammann*.

Morris came alongside early on, as noted, but the two ships rubbed and both suffered damage in the heavy swell and backed away.

Captain Lowry was ready to take the survivors and keep them, when the first signal from Admiral Fletcher had warned that *Lex's* fires were beyond control, Lowry had notified the supply officer that he had to get ready to receive at least a thousand survivors. He called the medical officer and told him what he must do.

Soon, as the men were still sliding down the lines of *Lexington*, every cot and every bit of bedding was being broken out aboard *Minneapolis*. The boats were out looking for survivors, and the ship's complement was ready for the job ahead.

Aboard the *Minneapolis* whaleboat, Captain Sherman looked back at his burning command. He was torn by mixed emotions. His crew had behaved magnificently and he was proud of them, from the moment the air strike was launched through the fighting of the ship, and the attempt to save her, and at this moment he still believed they had won a glorious victory over the Japanese. He was only sorry poor *Lexington* had to perish in her hour of glory. And yet, was it not better that she die thus rather than live on and end up on the scrap heap?

Darkness was nearing, and in the gloaming the fires above and inside *Lexington* burned redly with sheets of white flame flashing after each explosion. She was a beacon in the sea and she now began to cause Admiral Fletcher worry on a new score. If the ship continued to float she would be a fine propaganda prize at least, for the Japanese. Right now, she offered danger to the fleet because she was a target for submarines and even planes.

The ships moved away and stood off, counting their survivors. *New Orleans* had 43 officers and 537 men aboard, forty of them critically wounded. *Anderson* had seventeen officers and 360 men. *Hammann* had aboard 478 officers and men.

Dewey had rescued 120 officers and men, and *Phelps* had saved two boatloads, or about thirty of-

202

ficers and men, and *Morris* still had her 400 survivors.

Many of these men were now transferred to the cruisers *Minneapolis* and *Portland,* where they could be better accommodated and the wounded could have more extensive facilities than on the smaller ships. Admiral Fitch, Captain Sherman, Commander Seligman, and Lieutenant Williams all made their way to the *Minneapolis,* where they were welcomed and cheered by the men of the cruiser, along with some seven hundred other survivors of their ship.

Admiral Fletcher had left the question of rescue to Admiral Kinkaid. There had to be a final check. At 1810, after it had grown quite dark, Lieutenant Commander J.C. Daniel took a whaleboat from the destroyer *Phelps* and made that last check. He moved to a point directly under the port side of the burning carrier, unmindful of the constant stream of explosions of ammunition that were occurring above. He swept along that whole side, and then around the starboard as far as the smoke would let him go. He would not have been able to see, had he gone into it. *Lexington* was listing 30 degrees, her flight deck was aflame from stem to stern, and planes were teetering on the edge of the buckled deck, threatening to fall overboard on top of the whaleboat. Not a living soul could be seen on the ship or in the water around her.

Admiral Kinkaid then gave the order that put an end to *Lexington* that night.

"Detail one DD to sink *Lexington* with torpedoes, then rejoin promptly."

Phelps Captain Beck made ready to do the job. The torpedoes were put in the tubes and the torpedo officer went to his battle post. The destroyer moved through the choppy evening sea to a point 1560 yards off the port side of the carrier. The torpedo officer set his depth at fifty feet, since *Lexington* had a draft of forty-five feet and he wanted to blow the bottom out of her. The first torpedo was fired at 1915. It ran true and exploded against the port side of the ship, opposite the barbette of the old Number 1 turret. It seemed to have no effect at all, and Captain Beck realized that he should be firing at the starboard side of the ship, because of the list. But to do so would be to endanger the fleet, in case a torpedo porpoised and changed course. In these early days of the war American torpedoes were not so accurate that this problem did not have to be considered.

Five minutes later, *Phelps* fired her second torpedo. This one seemed to turn into the side amidships, but there was no explosion. It either missed—changed course, which American torpedoes were known to do—or the warhead was defective.

Nine more minutes . . . the third torpedo. This one did explode abreast her stack, and the effect was almost immediate. The carrier's list increased another ten degrees. But there she hung, still burning, still sending smoke and red flame up through the night air.

All this while, the ships of the fleet had been moving away from the area, to give *Phelps* full sway. *Lexington* was well down on her side, the port edge of the flight deck no longer fifty feet above water, but awash.

Lieutenant Commander Beck moved *Phelps* around to starboard and stood off the bow of the carrier. Here the destroyer fired her fourth torpedo, from 1200 yards out, again set at fifty feet. The torpedo disappeared in the smoke that covered the ship on this side, and the sound of explosion was heard. But still *Lexington* did not sink.

Now it was 1952. *Phelps* had been trying to sink the stubborn Queen of the Flat-tops for more than half an hour. But although she could not live, it was hard for her to die. The torpedo officer set the depth for a fifth torpedo at thirty feet, and at 1952 he fired it off. But just as he fired, *Lexington* disappeared in the smoke. The darkness and the smoke cloud were so thick that no one on *Phelps* saw her go, no one could tell if she capsized, or sank stern to, or simply went down.

Thirty seconds later came a tremendous explosion, immediately followed by another, so earth-shaking that other ships of the task force, ten miles away, were also shocked by it. Aboard *Phelps* the effect seemed catastrophic. Captain Beck believed he had been torpedoed by a Japanese submarine. (Almost precisely this was to happen a month later to an American destroyer trying to succor *Yorktown* in the Battle of Midway). Captain Alexander Early, Commander of Destroyer Squadron One, who was aboard *Phelps*, believed depth charges had somehow been dropped by the destroyer and that she had blown up.

Captain Early got on the RBS and called the task force: *Phelps* HAS HAD A SERIOUS EXPLOSION. STAND BY TO GIVE ASSISTANCE. STERN BELIEVED TO BE BLOWN OFF.

But examination revealed no damage, other than the shock itself, and the commander of the squadron got back on the radio, and called off the alert.

What had occurred were two last violent explosions on *Lexington* as she went down. Either bombs were thrown against red hot metal, or steam pressure was so great that when the cold saltwater hit the red-hot steal, she blew. In any event, she sank, down to the bottom, in 2400 fathoms, at Lat. 15°12' South, Long. 155°27' East. Her heroic life had ended.

Chapter Eighteen

The Ordeal of *Neosho* -IV

Night fell a hundred miles south of the task force. The sea was quiet, except for the hum of the waves and the whisper of the wind, which sent a chill through the men clustered on the port deck of the wrecked tanker. This list was still 30 degrees, but had grown no more severe in the last twelve hours.

All day long they had tried, and failed, to get a reliable sight for navigation purposes. Now not even a star helped them. They must wait until the moon came up and the stars came out, or for the next day.

The men were exhausted, red-eyed and sunburned. The exposure and the salt had cracked their lips and lined their eyes. They were unshaven and grimy, but those who were unhurt could look over at the still forms of the burned and wounded on the deck and be glad they were in one piece. There was water, there was food, but there was also this night the terrible uncertainty that had dogged them as the day wore on, and the captain discovered that the wrong fix had been given to Task Force 17 before they began their rescue operations. Would they ever be found?

Captain Phillips decided that night that he must be prepared to save himself and his crew; that the chances of Task Force 17 reaching them were diminishing at every moment. So that night he called his navigator and the chief engineer and they made plans for the following day.

And the rest of the crew slumped on the deck, or lay on the steel plates, moving restlessly. And waited.

Chapter Nineteen

Retirement

Admiral Fletcher had been undecided as to whether he should stage a night attack or retire. Admiral Nimitz, in Pearl Harbor, decided it for him; late in the day he ordered Fletcher to retire from the Coral Sea. So the Task Force set its course southward, coming closer to the wreck of *Neosho* that night, but totally unmindful of her.

Admiral Inouye at Rabaul postponed the Port Moresby invasion indefinitely. He ordered the transport group, carrying the soldiers and their supplies, to come back to Rabaul. He was concerned about the American carrier that might still be left in operation, and about the increased activity of General MacArthur's land-based air searches these past few days. With *Shoho* sunk, and *Shokaku* dispatched homeward, vitally injured, the admiral did not feel it wise to risk the invasion forces.

Further the fuel situation was not good. Although Japanese army forces had overrun the Dutch oil fields in the East Indies with remarkable ease, and there had been virtually no sabotage, still the supply people had not managed yet to set up adequate surpluses down here in the south. The movement had simply been too rapid. So Admiral Inouye was dogged by the old familiar sailor's complaint—fuel worries—and he let them determine his course of action. The cruisers and destroyers of the invasion force were sent north to fuel, and be on the alert. The striking force—Admiral Takagi's unit, which included carrier *Zuikaku*—was ordered back towards Truk, where the admiral could replenish his fuel supplies and take on new planes to replace those destroyed in the fight against the Americans. The whole operation was then abandoned, and Admiral Inouye concentrated on his next move, which was to be the occupation of Ocean and Nauru islands.

When Admiral Yamamoto, commander in chief of the Combined Fleet, learned of Inouye's decision, he was furious, and he stopped his planning for the coming battle of Midway long enough to order Takagi to return to the Coral Sea and wipe out the American forces remaining there. So after midnight a confused Takagi responded to the new orders, and turned around, having been steaming north steadily for the past eight hours. Admiral Takagi knew he had virtually no chance of finding Admiral Fletcher by this time, but Yamamoto was the commander in chief, and there was no arguing with him.

The Twenty-Fifty Air Flotilla got its orders that night. At dawn the planes were to be out, searching for the carrier force or its remnants, and the bombers were to "annihilate" the enemy.

That night, then, both forces were still thinking about another fight, but not very seriously.

Admiral Fletcher was glad enough. He had only eight fighters, twelve bombers, and eight torpedo planes available and ready for action, and only seven torpedoes left for the planes, after three days of action. He had not wanted to make a day surface attack because of the existence of that uninjured carrier that Admiral Fitch had noted. As the force headed southward, he began a ship-by-ship check of the damage.

The admiral had taken back tactical command of the force with the troubles of *Lexington*, after the Japanese attack had ended. He had been hoping, almost until the last, to take *Lexington*'s serviceable planes aboard *Yorktown* and send *Lex* back to Pearl Harbor for repairs. Those hopes went down with the ship. Now he had nothing to do but go back to Noumea and resupply, ream, and see what Nimitz wanted next.

In retrospect that evening, Admiral Fletcher could be pleased with his decision. Had he done otherwise he might have left *Lexington* only with a small screen and it was questionable if the destroyers alone would have been able to save the whole crew of *Lexington*, as the whole force did. The total casualties of the ship, from the fight against the Japanese and the fight against the sea, had been only eight percent. Many other lives would have been lost if the whole attack group had not been around to help in *Lexington*'s hour of need.

In a sense, *Minneapolis* that night became the center of attraction of the task force. When Correspondent Johnston walked into the wardroom of the cruiser that evening, he was surprised. The whole wardroom of *Lexington* seemed to have been transported there.

The ship had quarters for an admiral, so Admiral Fitch and his staff had no problem at all about accommodations. Captain Lowry took Captain Sherman into his quarters; the executive officer of the *Minneapolis* shared with Commander Seligman, and the chief engineer with *Lex*'s Chief Engineer Junkers. In every place where there was a counterpart, the officers shared. As for the men, the sailors of *Minneapolis* gave up their bunks, using the hot bunk technique—a man on watch doubling with his counterpart who was off—so that many of *Lexington*'s men were accommodated. Then cots were broken out for the fliers and the sailors who could not be given bunks, and when the cots ran out, mattresses were put down on deck.

Lieutenant Roach, who had been exhausted by a lengthy stay in the water, and unsuccessful attempts to swim away from the ship's side, no sooner got aboard *Minneapolis* than he set up a sick bay and insisted on going right to work.

Lieutenant Williams, the paymaster, no sooner set foot on the deck of the cruiser than he was worrying about how to straighten out his records. That very night he went to the supply officer Lieutenant Commander John DeWitt, and got his help in running off a sample form for sworn statements, so the men could get paid. Pay books lost (except for Williams's squadrons) the men might wait months for the red tape to be cleared up in Washington, and conceivably, if they were transferred to active units in the fleet, it would take months for them to get any money again.

How DeWitt found time to even talk to anyone seemed a minor miracle. He had been given the word at 1500 to prepare to take on 1200 survivors, feed them two hot meals a day, keep hot coffee going at all times, follow his planned menus, and not cause anybody any trouble.

He had worked, and his officers and men had worked steadily until the survivors came aboard, and had the hot meal ready: frankfurters and sauerkraut, spareribs, fruit salad, potatoes, bread and butter, and coffee. He started feeding at 1645, but did not manage to hold it down to two hours, since survivors were still coming aboard at 1915. And then, in spite of all his efforts, half the men were too exhausted, or had swallowed too much of the Coral Sea, to eat at all. But they did away that night with 320 gallons of coffee.

The galley was hot from that time on around the clock, with two men on night duty, and both watches working almost continually from 0330 to 1900. In the bake shop the men went on 24 hour watches, one group working 24 hours, and then going off for 24.

The result was an unprecedented smooth flow in a time of great stress. All the difference it seemed to make in the menu was that the coconut cookies had to be deleted from the menu one day, and apple pie another. There was just too much pressure on the bake shop, for the men of *Lexington* to have a rescue and apple pie as well.

As night closed in, DeWitt made a head count. He had about 700 survivors aboard. Many of them were in soaking clothing and some were naked. But the line was formed to the supply-issue room, and as the men came up they got underwear and shoes and toilet articles.

DeWitt, who had given up his bunk to Correspondent Johnston, sat up late reading the navy regulations about shipwrecked mariners, to see what he could do with what he had, without facing court-martial for misuse of government property.

All night long the American task force steamed south. Next morning the course was changed towards the rising sun, which would lead them into the friendly waters of New Caledonia and Tonga. Admiral Fletcher was going to send the cruisers *Minneapolis*, *New Orleans* and *Astoria*, with four destroyers, into Noumea. The rest of the force would go to Tongatubu to resupply.

On the morning of May 9, Fletcher was still ready to fight, although his air power was greatly diminished. A scout plane reported an aircraft carrier 175 miles away, and dive bombers went out to get it, joined by army bombers called from an Australian air base. But the carrier turned out to be a flat reef, not a ship.

Admiral Takagi was searching for the American task force in the southern waters, but he turned southwest, which took him in the opposite direction.

Up north, Admiral Halsey was steaming down from Pearl Harbor, with a whole new task force, including carriers *Enterprise* and *Hornet*, to try to join the battle. But the forces were drawing too far apart for this. On the morning of May 9, the army air forces from Australia began plastering DeBoyne Island, and the Japanese seaplane base there. They knocked out most of the planes, and the base was abandoned.

The first word of the battle was coming out in the press of America and of Japan. The New York *Times* called the battle a great American victory, with 17 of 22 Japanese ships sunk, and painted a picture of the American task force vigorously pursuing the battered remnants of the Japanese force. This claim went much further than Admiral Fletcher's. He estimated that the planes of Task Force 17 had sunk two destroyers, three cargo ships, four gunboats, one light cruiser, one light carrier, various gunboats and other small craft, and caused one light cruiser to beach itself. He also estimated that his men had damaged a destroyer, another heavy cruiser, and carrier *Shokaku*, all seriously. They had, he said, also slightly damaged carrier *Zuikaku*. They had destroyed three torpedo bombers off Port Moresby, five sea planes, three patrol bombers, seven fighters, fourteen torpedo bombers in the air—in all, 144 Japanese planes. Japanese personnel losses were put at 5100.

Admiral Fletcher knew what American losses were:

one carrier, one destroyer and one tanker sunk, and one carrier damaged. Fifteen *Lexington* planes had been lost in combat, and 35 had gone down with the ship. Sixteen *Yorktown* planes had been lost in combat. In all the Americans had lost 66 planes and an estimated 543 men.

The Japanese were equally vehement in claiming a total victory. On the morning of May 9, Sergeant Kawakami and his men were busy under the hot Java sun moving naval prisoners to a new barracks, now that the Javanese had mostly been released. He took time to listen to the radio, however, and heard Tokyo broadcast that Japan had thoroughly defeated a British fleet off the coast of New Guinea. The first reports were obviously fragmentary, but Radio Tokyo assured the Japanese people it was the greatest victory since Pearl Harbor. Sergeant Kawakami was proud and a little relieved, for he had been worrying about overextension of the empire.

The elation in the United States was somewhat tempered on the evening of May 9, when the Japanese announced the sinking of Admiral Crace's force, expanded by Domei, the Imperial News Agency, to include a number of battleships and both American carriers. The New York *Times* called for caution in believing the Japanese claims, but ran no more headlines announcing a huge victory. Correspondents of the American press began hounding the Navy Department for more information.

But Admiral King in Washington and Admiral Nimitz in Pearl Harbor were tight-lipped. They knew of something the correspondents did not even guess—that as Admiral Fletcher steamed toward Tongatubu, the Japanese were massing in the home waters for a huge new naval strike elsewhere. New York *Times* military analyst Hanson W. Baldwin assessed the

214

King-Nimitz fears perhaps unintentionally, when he referred in one of his articles to the seven-ocean war being fought by America's one-ocean navy. King and Nimitz were delaying any official report on the Battle of the Coral Sea so they would give no valuable information to the Japanese enemy. America's shortage of ships, and particularly carriers, was so desperate that even the question of one carrier's existence was important in assessment of the situation. So Washington and Pearl Harbor were silent.

On *Minneapolis* and the other ships, the supply officers were almost as busy as the captains these days. Lieutenant Commander DeWitt authorized the issuance of a set of underwear, a pair of shoes, socks, shirt, trousers and a towel to every *Lexington* survivor. The men of the other ships also turned to help out their shipwrecked comrades, with razors and toilet equipment and other clothing. On the morning of May 9, the men of *Minneapolis* came to a breakfast of figs, pork and beans, bacon, and hot corn bread. Lunch was bean soup, baked ham, raisin sauce, potatoes, carrots, onions and dill pickles. There was scarcely an outward sign of any difficulty at all.

As the ships steamed toward harbor, the medical officers of the various rescue vessels were tending their charges. Commander H.A. Gross, chief medical officer of the *Minneapolis*, took over the Marine compartment to house the *Lexington* men suffering from immersion, exhaustion and mild shock. Just going into the water and trying to swim, even though it had been quite warm, had done in many men, and some were half-drowned from swimming in the heavy sea.

But surgeon Gross's real worry was in sick bay, where he housed the seriously wounded and the burned. For the burned it was tannic acid treatment and transfusions of whole blood or plasma. There was one really desperate case: Yeoman Third Class Harry Daniel Ziegler had suffered terrible third-degree burns, and was unconscious on arrival. Dr. Gross had hope; Ziegler responded to shock therapy and a plasma transfusion. Other badly burned men were Fireman First Class Julian K. Johnston, Matt 1 c Leland P. Sheldon, and Sk 3 c Robert D. Zaniboni. There were some 250 hurt men, but only ten badly enough injured to be on the sick list. All went well, except for Yeoman Ziegler. He never regained consciousness, and died early on the morning of May 9.

That morning, Admiral Fitch, Captain Sherman, and Commander Seligman came down to sick bay and visited the sick and wounded, and talked a little with the men in the Marine compartment. They were proud of the men of *Lexington*, and they had a right to be.

Aboard destroyers and the other cruisers it was about the same pattern. One man died shortly after coming aboard. Two more died that night, and, like Yeoman Ziegler, they were buried at sea with full military honors. The doctors worked hard to save others. One man on *New Orleans* had flash burns, he had inhaled salt water and developed pneumonia, and that first night he ran a temperature of 106°. It stayed right there, almost up to 107° for forty-eight hours. But with transfusions and sulfa and warm care, it began to come down.

Chaplain Markle was aboard *New Orleans*, and he did what he could to comfort the men, although he had had quite a shock himself. He had gone over the side and tried to swim away from the ship, but the suction was very strong, and by the time he could get out from under the overhang and see blue sky, he was tired. Luckily, a raft full of men came drifting by, and the other survivors pulled him aboard. They drifted until the boat from *New Orleans* picked them off the raft. The chaplain went aboard, and what he wanted most was a shower, to scrub away the encrustation of fuel oil that had clung to him from *Lexington's* leaking tanks as he swam. Out of the shower, he was given a pair of blue dungarees and a blue shirt, and one last look at the tower of smoke 200 feet in the air, and the bright red glow beneath that was *Lexington*, before she sank. Then, Chaplain Markle realized how shaken he really was, as he turned to his work of compassion.

Chapter Twenty

The Ordeal of *Neosho*-V

There were no showers aboard *Neosho* to which the oil-soaked men could turn. There was no chaplain there to offer them solace or hope, and on the morning of May 9, hope was what the survivors of the two ships needed, if they were to face the Coral Sea sun and the wind and waves.

Captain Phillips set about trying to instil that hope. He was badly shaken by the realization that Admiral Fletcher's rescuers had gone out with wrong information. It could well mean the difference between life and death to them all. But he was not ready to give up. Early in the morning, the pharmacists came to him to report three more men had died: Fireman Third Class Davis A. Christian, Fireman First Class Henry T. Chapman, Chief Construction Mechanic Benjamin F. Baggarly, all from *Neosho*. Preparations were made to bury them at sea.

The captain estimated that they were heading northwest with the current, at about 1.4 knots. There were two possibilities of survival, and they both depended on the men of *Neosho*. First was to get an accurate fix of position, which could be sent on the auxiliary radio. That task was given Lieutenant Brown, the gunnery officer, and he set to work. The alternative was to take to the boats and try to make a landfall. Lieutenant Verbrugge had been studying the problem of loosing the Number 2 motor launch, and he reported to the captain that he thought he could do it without power if he could have some men. Captain Phillips gave him the job.

Meanwhile, every effort had to be made to keep the hulk of *Neosho* floating and as stable as possible. Down below, the men found some hacksaws, and began the laborious process of sawing through the anchor chain, so the starboard anchor could be jettisoned and the dragging weight removed. They were still canted over with a list of about 24 degrees to starboard. The men sawed and sawed, until blisters reddened their hands, and finally the chain gave. With a heavy clanking, the steel links banged against the hull, and then disappeared. Anchor and 165 fathoms of chain went down. Disappointingly, the change in the list was very slight, evidence of the mortal wounds *Neosho* had suffered below the water line. It was proof to Captain Phillips that the ship could not last much longer.

At 1012 Lieutenant Brown took his first sighting, and reported a position: Latitude 15°35″ South, and Longitude 156°55′ East. By Captain Phillips's calculation, they had drifted almost a degree of latitude to the north and more than a degree to the west in the past forty-eight hours.

In midmorning, Lieutenant Verbrugge began rigging tackle and chain hoists to the davits of Number 2 motor launch. Other men were put to work again this day making floats and rafts of every available object that would offer flotation. The captain was now almost certain their only salvation would be to abandon ship and set out for land. Junior officers were set to rigging all boats with masts, spars, and sails, and making sure they were as watertight as possible, and that the provisions would be ready to go into them.

The captain now was making final preparations for abandoning the ship. The list had returned to 23 degrees to starboard, even after jettisoning the anchor. That was not very good, and the decks were taking water, the upper deck on the starboard side was awash. A really heavy storm might well sink them in a few minutes.

The funeral services brought all hands to the side of the ship while Captain Phillips said the prayer and the bodies were sent down into the deep. Then the men went back to work, sober, but given hope by the determined buoyancy of their captain and officers. Lieutenant Verbrugge, by midday, had the motor launch almost clear of the skids. Lieutenant Brown took another sighting at 1300 and found that they were still drifting northwest, perhaps a little faster than before.

The pharmacists were still treating their burned men, but there was not much they could do, except ease the pain of the worst, and be sure the bandages were clean and the wounds kept covered.

The captain was taking stock. Of the three motor whale boats in the water, the engine in only one, the gig, was working. So it was going to have to be by sailing if they were to make it to land. The other two boats were attached to the gig for towing and they all stayed in close to the *Neosho*. It was no time for anyone to get lost.

As night fell and Lieutenant Verbrugge came wearily to report to the captain on his progress. He could say that the Number 2 boat was now clear of the skids, and halfway over toward the port side of the ship.

After dark, Lieutenant Brown took another fix, this time on the stars, and found that they were still drifting, but now southwest. The sea was still rough, and the wind continued. At nightfall, the men of *Neosho* settled down, wondering if anyone was really looking for them, and if they would ever find this little speck of steel floating in the Coral Sea.

But out there, hundreds of miles away, the search was going on. Vice Admiral H. F. Leary had learned that *Monaghan* had found nothing, and he had detailed the PBY's stationed at Noumea to make a serious search for the survivors. The flying boats were taking off and landing all day long, making their long searches, but they found nothing. *Tangier*, the seaplane carrier, was in charge of the job. Then, on the night of May 8, Captain L. B. Austin, Commander of Destroyer Division Seven, embarked in the destroyer *Henley* to go to the scene of the attack, as reported uncorrected, to try to find the survivors or get some indication of what had happened. At 0800 on the morning of May 9, as the men of *Neosho* were turning to their tasks for the day, *Henley* steamed out of Noumea, passing *Flusser*, which was just entering port. Captain Austin told Commander Robert Hall Smith to set course and head for Latitude 16°—15° South, 157° East. Commander Smith ordered 20 knots and a zigzag pattern as they went, and they headed out. All day long they steamed, and at dark they cut back to 15 knots for the night. They were heading toward the *Neosho,* until midnight, when Captain Austin had the report that an enemy carrier was supposedly located at 17° 30′ South and 152° 30″ East, on course 110. He ordered Commander Smith to turn away to a course of 130° to miss the carrier, if she was indeed there, and *Henley* moved back away from the *Neosho* at fifteen knots.

Chapter Twenty-one

The Last of the *Neosho*

The Japanese were jubilant. After that first spate of exuberant publicity in the American press, with its exorbitant claims of sinkings, there simply was no more news from the American front, and in Tokyo this meant the enemy must have suffered a desperate loss. Official congratulations were passing around Tokyo like rice cakes. The Emperor gave personal congratulations in the form of an Imperial Rescript to Admiral Yamamoto. Premier Tojo added his appreciation to the fleet for "wiping out the main units of the British and American combined fleet in the Coral Sea." And the Japanese navy added a destroyer, a cruiser, and a tanker to their list of carriers and battleships and cruisers already "sunk" in the fight.

Admiral Takagi continued to search for the Americans until May 10. Then he turned around and headed for Truk, and passed out of the Coral Sea where he had found nothing more.

Japanese land-based airplanes continued their search for the American force, but they were not flying in the direction of Noumea; it was a long haul for them. Nineteen search planes were out and 14 Zeros attacked Port Moresby. But the invasion was off, and the planes not concentrated their efforts against submarines that were bothering Japanese shipping around Tulagi and Rabaul. On May 10, Admiral

Inouye ordered the seaplane tender to move out of DeBoyne Island's base, and return to Rabaul. He was going to concentrate all his attention to Nauru and Ocean Islands, which were next on the occupation list.

Aboard *Minneapolis* Admiral Fitch and Captain Sherman and Executive officer Seligman were busy putting together their reports of the action they had just been through. It was essential that these be prepared for Admiral Nimitz as soon as possible. Lieutenant Williams was busy, too, running off thousands of copies of the forms he wanted his men to fill out so they could get back on the Navy payroll.

Had Captain Phillips of *Neosho* known of these concerns he would have thought them very small potatoes indeed, for he and his men were facing the stark problems of survival.

On the morning of May 10, the pharmacists came up again with their doleful news: Seaman Second Class Noel E. Craven and Seaman First Class Hugh T. Gonia, and Matt Second Class Willie Coates had died of their wounds and must be buried that morning.

The hulk of *Neosho* was drifting as she had been, going this way and that in the trade wind's path, but generally moving westward slowly and steadily. The list was still 23 degrees; the cutting of the anchor had not helped. The upper deck was down a little lower in the water this morning than it had been the night before. Slowly, very slowly, they were sinking, and at some point the ship would give a lurch, a gurgle, and go down. Captain Phillips task was to be sure the officers and men of *Neosho* were not aboard when that happened.

Insofar as abandoning ship was concerned, good progress was made this day. Lieutenant Verbrugge got the motor launch over the port side and into the water without swamping. Then he began loading her with supplies. With the funeral, the work of loading, and the general cleanup that must be done every morning to keep the men occupied and the ship as sanitary as possible, the time passed until noon. At 1230 someone heard a buzzing, and looking up, saw a speck in the sky south of them. The speck moved up and became a plane, and as it came close to the ship, it was identified as an Australian Hudson. Quickly the signal searchlight was hooked up to the auxiliary generator and the signalman sent a message identifying *Neosho*. Captain Phillips ordered men to hoist the international distress signal and the international call. The Hudson responded—blinked back to ask if the ship was in trouble. It certainly was, said Captain Phillips. He tried to give the latest position, which had been estimated by the gunnery officer early that morning as 15° 55.5′ South. 156° 17′ East. Several times that information was blinked out as the Hudson circled, but there was no response to indicate that it had been received or would bring action.

After circling again, the Hudson turned and disappeared toward the south. Soon even the sound was gone, and the men of *Neosho* were again alone with the sea, the sun, and the heavy swell of the trade-wind latitudes.

But there was cause for rejoicing. It seemed almost certain that something was going to happen soon. There was no doubt about the existence of the Hudson. There was no doubt, either, that they had been seen, and had engaged in blinker conversation, and that the Hudson crew knew they were an allied ship in sore distress. Certainly the Australians would communicate with MacArthur, and he with Pearl Harbor, and someone would be coming to get them.

To celebrate, Captain Phillips ordered the hot plates rigged up to the auxiliary generator, which he had not done before because he had felt the need to conserve every bit of energy for the dispatch of messages. Now with the vital message received, perhaps they could relax a bit. So this day the men had the first hot coffee they had enjoyed since the Japanese came zooming down on them four days before.

Captain Phillips knew, nonetheless, that he could not relax completely. They still must be prepared at a moment's notice to abandon the ship and take to the boats, lest Neosho sink under them. The preparations continued.

That afternoon work crews took the engines out of one of Neosho's motor whale boats and the Sims boat, for the two were both damaged and would not run. They only added unwanted weight that could much better be supplied by men than machines. A party went aft to measure the fresh water supply. That, at least, was in abundance, for no damage had been done to the tanks. All available containers were filled and stowed in the boats. Ship's service stores were raided under the eye of the assistant supply officer, and the fruit juices were all taken aboard the boats, too. The supply officer then set about rationing out the food supply among the boats, and it was packed.

Captain Phillips worked out the final assignment of men to boats, taking into consideration the wounded and the number of able-bodied, who must be distributed evenly. He also drew up a list of items to be checked off before they abandoned.

The captain had decided now that unless they were found by the next day, he would abandon ship, and make for the nearest land. It was certainly a better course than to sit here, losing strength, the wounded dying, the burned not getting any better, and wasting away the supplies that might take them home again.

The Number 2 motor launch that Lieutenant Verbrugge had salvaged was to be the key to the whole effort. It would be used to tow the other three whale boats. And by a little cramming, everyone could be accommodated in the four boats. The captain and Lieutenant Brown pulled out all the charts they had. They made a full study of the South Pacific Pilot Chart and Coast Pilot, and put all the charts and navigation equipment they would need in the Number 2 boat. The captain laid out a course to Willis Island, where they would stop if possible, and then head through Trinity Opening to Cairns Harbor, on the Australian coast. Lieutenant Brown then checked the boat compass for deviation from true readings. When the Number 2 boat was equipped, remaining navigational equipment was divided among the other boats. In case they should be separated by storm or other disaster each boat should be ready to try to go it alone.

A few hundred miles away, the destroyer *Henley* was again steaming toward the last reported position of *Neosho*. All night long she had fled the supposed Japanese carrier force, but at dawn she had turned about, and headed back whence she had come, having lost a good six hours. Recognizing the need for haste, Captain Austin had increased the speed to 20 knots as night fell, and later that night of May 10 he raised it to 25 knots.

Night brought its black worries to the men of *Neosho* once again. All day long the deck had kept buckling a little more each watch, and it was especially notable on the main-deck plating abaft the bridge. Captain Phillips sent Lieutenant Verbrugge below, and he came to report that the water level in the

226

fireroom and in the main engineroom had increased remarkably. It was up three feet in the engine room from the day before, and up seven feet in the fire room. So Captain Phillips felt that tomorrow, the 11th of May, was the fatal day on which they must cast their lot with the sea. It seemed a fair chance that the ship would hold together during the night, the weather staying calm. But to expect much more would be to ask for miracles, and the captain had stopped doing that.

Among the men, the night of May 10 was a time of despair. It was certain that the rescue attempts had either not been made or had failed. There was no reason, given receipt and understanding of the messages, that the Task Force should not have reached them by this time—no reason except the faulty position given by the navigator in his carelessness.

So the night passed. The morning of May 11 saw *Henley* moving to the last reported position of *Neosho*. At 0630 *Henley* changed her base course to 296°. At 0735 she changed course to 273°. At 0920 she changed to 290°.

Ten minutes later *Henley* passed an oil slick at Lat 16° 07′ South, Long. 156° 15′ East. Captain Austin and the men of the ship felt they must be coming close to the oiler.

At 1009, however, they passed the last reported position of the *Neosho* and found nothing but a vast expanse of empty sea before them.

Captain Austin then began to consider the possible direction of drift of the *Neosho* and came to the conclusion that she must drifting northwest, so changed course to follow that assumption. At 1115 a PBY came by and joined the search, using *Henley* as a base point. Not quite an hour later the plane returned to report that the *Neosho* was just fifty miles away, bearing 033 degrees from the ship.

Aboard *Neosho*, Captain Phillips was making ready to abandon the hulk. Early in the morning, Gunnery Officer Brown had taken his sights, while other officers checked the ship for seaworthiness. They reported to Captain Phillips that although the list had decreased, the reason for it was the settling of the ship deeper in the water. The after end had gone down very appreciably in the past twenty-four hours. The plates forward had begun to buckle and the plates of the main deck just abaft the bridge were much worse. The captain decided to make an effort, now that the ship was so much closer to the water, to hoist over the Number 1 motor launch. In any event, he was now determined that they would abandon at the first sign of movement. He feared that at almost any time the *Neosho* would sink or break in half.

In mid-morning, Captain Phillips called a conference of all the officers. As they gathered around him, he laid out the plan for them. By best estimate, they were 540 miles from the Australian coast. He assigned each officer to his boat and function, and then gave detailed orders. No personal possessions would be allowed in the boats. There was no room. The officers adjourned, and the captain busied himself with last-minute details. Undoubtedly that afternoon, they would abandon ship.

But at 1130, a speck appeared high above the horizon, and the droning noise of airplane engines rumbled across the sea. There was always the gut reaction: was it one of theirs or one of ours? But as the plane approached, it was identified as a PBY, an American Navy flying boat. It came up, circled *Neosho* twice, and then flew away to the south. Hope rose in the hearts of the shipwrecked men, cautious hope.

The day before they had seen a plane and nothing had come of it that they could see. They did not know that the Hudson's report had been sent along, and furnished part of the information on which Captain Austin and the PBY were acting. They could not know. They could only hope and wait.

A long hour passed, and then another half hour. Suddenly someone started and shouted.

"A ship!"

They watched her come up on the horizon from the south, again half apprehensive as to whether she was American or Japanese. But the familiar outlines of an American destroyer made themselves clear through the glass, and finally she was identified as *Henley*, a ship they knew well.

At 1323 *Henley* approached, and Captain Phillips began signalling:

HAVE YOU ANY INSTRUCTIONS FOR ME. SHIP IS A TOTAL LOSS, SETTLING GRADUALLY. WHAT ARE YOUR ORDERS?

Captain Austin sent back:

NO ORDERS

Captain Phillips then began reporting the number of survivors, as *Henley* crossed the stern of the tanker, and her men began heaving lines on the port side.

Captain Austin broke in:

EXPEDITE TRANSFER OF SURVIVORS

There would be plenty of time later to get all the details. Now it was time to get the men off the wreck. Captain Austin did not relish being hove to in the middle of what might be a very unfriendly ocean, full of Japanese submarines, the skies perhaps laden with Japanese planes heading toward him and he at a standstill.

He sent up the flat hoist

EMERG VICTOR

Which meant emergency, in simple language, and get to it, in navy shorthand.

Captain Phillips got the message. The men were herded aboard the *Henley* just as quickly as possible, not being given time even to go to the boats and get whatever personal gear they had temporarily left there. Captain Austin was in a hurry and he was nervous. As the whaleboats came alongside and the men were transferred, he ordered the boats scuttled.

At 1415, Captain Phillips herded the last man into the last boat and stepped off his command. The boat went to the side of *Henley,* and the last of 109 survivors of *Neosho* and 14 survivors of *Sims* went aboard. The whale boat could not be scuttled, so it was set adrift.

Captains Austin and Phillips conferred. The oiler skipper said *Neosho* was unsalvageable, and Captain Austin believed he knew whereof he spoke, for Phillips had spent four days with not so much more to do than observe the changing character of his command. So *Henley* set about sinking the ship.

She fired one torpedo at 1428, but it did not explode—another negative tribute to the false economy of the American defense effort in the years before the war. For while the Japanese navy was developing the famous long-lance torpedo by the process of trial and error—exploding torpedoes against targets to see what happened, the American Navy was not allowed to use real warheads. In war games the torpedoes were always dummies, and warheads were conserved. Congress wanted it that way. But the result had been the development of American torpedoes that did not explode, that did not run true, that did virtually no good at all. This torpedo fired at 1428 was one of them, a waste of $10,000 of the taxpayers' money.

Two minutes later *Henley* fired another torpedo,

and this one hit the hulk amidships. But still she did not go down. The destroyer then opened up with five-inch shells, and fired 146 rounds before the *Neosho* finally sank, stern first.

Then *Henley* moved away, setting a course that would follow the apparent drift track of *Neosho* in reverse, in an effort to find and rescue the hundred and fifty men who had panicked and abandoned ship in the first few minutes after the Japanese attack. The men of *Neosho* and *Sims* who had followed the rule of the sea and stuck with the wreck were saved.

Chapter Twenty-two

The Change in the Tide

By May 12, Radio Tokyo was absolutely jubilant about the events that had occurred in the Coral Sea during the week. Imperial Headquarters issued its first official communiqué concerning the battle and it seemed to prove everything that the news agancies had been claiming all along.

In the great naval battle of the Coral Sea on 7th and 8th May the Japanese fleet succeeded in sinking the American *Saratoga* and the *Yorktown* class and capital ship of the *California* class, a British warship of the *Warspite* class; a cruiser of the *Canberra* class was severely damaged; another cruiser sunk, a 20,000 ton oil tanker sunk, and a destroyer sunk. Planes destroyed were 98. Japanese losses were negligible—1 small aircraft carrier converted from a tanker and 31 planes.

What the Japanese said was highly exaggerated as far as the Americans were concerned, obviously, and highly downgraded as far as the Japanese were concerned. But from the face of it, the fight did appear to be a Japanese victory. The Imperial Navy had sunk one American fleet carrier and damaged another, sunk an oiler and sunk a destroyer, while losing only *Shoho* and a large number of planes, and suffering severe enough damage to *Shokaku* to keep her out of the war for several months. It was a tactical victory.

But strategically—it was something else again.

Admiral Fitch, the American air commander, summed up his impressions in his action report. He thought at the time that *Shokaku* must have sunk, so he, too, regarded the affair as an American victory, even though *Lexington* had gone down.

Admiral Fitch had learned a great deal about air warfare in this first great carrier battle. The navy had to get better fighters and more of them, and better torpedo planes, and get them fast. Further, the fighter directors had to keep those combat air patrols up high, at 20,000 feet. Had the American patrol been at 20,000 feet instead of 10,000 when the Japanese were first sighted, the effect of their attack might have been better blunted. As it was the fighters completely missed the first Japanese wave. And as defense against torpedo planes, dive bombers were just not good enough.

Admiral Fitch gave the Japanese their due. The two carriers he faced were superior in number of fighters, in performance of the fighters, and in torpedo planes. So that meant the Americans absolutely must solve the plane and torpedo problems if they were to win the war.

As for Admiral Takagi, he had for the first time met the Americans in a real battle, and had learned that they could fight. The Japanese had gone into Coral Sea victims of their own propaganda about the decadent westerners. They had come out chastened, with the pilots who came back from the raid on the American carriers reporting how tough the Americans could be and how devastating their anti-aircraft fire had been.

To the Japanese public of course not a word of this

came through. But events were proving that the high command had learned suddenly to respect the enemy.

Admiral Inouye was going ahead with his invasion of Nauru and Ocean Islands, and on May 10 the ships set out, augmented by strength from the abortive Port Moresby invasion, which was now delayed indefinitely. But the flagship of the Nauru fleet, *Okinoshima*, was ambushed by the American submarine *S-42* and sunk, and then came a frightening report: two American carriers and a number of support ships were sighted by patrol planes 450 miles east of Tulagi. The Americans were coming again in great force! Admiral Inouye cancelled the Nauru invasion for the moment, and ordered the fleet into the safety of the big naval base at Truk.

Admiral Fitch also noted in his Action Report that the Japanese were superior in the use of shore-based aircraft, and recommended that additional U.S. planes be brought to the Southwest Pacific to cooperate with the naval units. This recommendation was to bring the admiral a new job, for having had his carrier shot out from under him, there was going to be a question as to how he might best be employed. At Pearl Harbor, Admiral Nimitz would very soon make Fitch director of land-based aircraft in the South Pacific area.

Back at Pearl Harbor, Admiral Nimitz and his staff were piecing together radio intelligence reports. Lieutenant Commander Edwin T. Layton, the fleet intelligence officer, had managed to break the Japanese naval code, so valuable information was coming through which indicated a Japanese attack in the central and western Pacific. Nimitz was not quite sure where, for the Japanese used a code name for the place. Since that was an arbitrary name there was no way of "cracking" it. Nimitz caused a message to be sent "in the clear" noting that Midway was short of water. In a few hours the Japanese were informing their fleet that the place to be attacked was short of water. So Nimitz knew.

His next action then, was to call Halsey and his two carriers back immediately from the South Pacific and to hurry Fletcher home to have *Yorktown* repaired of the damage caused by the Japanese bombs.

For three days *Henley* searched for the four officers and 154 men who had disappeared on the rafts when *Neosho* was attacked, but she found nothing. She then headed for Brisbane.

As *Henley* searched, the men aboard the rafts were dying, one by one. Some rafts had managed to stick together, with 64 men clinging to them, and they headed for Noumea, where they would find safety. But the officers who had been so quick to abandon ship were deficient in other attributes, and discipline almost immediately broke down. What supplies they had were quickly consumed without stiff rationing. Men dying of thirst drank sea water, and died more quickly. Men gnawed with hunger quarreled and lost their strength. The officers who might have given them hope were no better leaders than the men.

Destroyer *Phelps* was dispatched from Noumea, and she conducted a search of her own. Three days out of Noumea, guided by Captain Phillips's replotting of the point where the attack had taken place, *Phelps* came upon four rafts lashed together. Four men were alive on these rafts—all that remained of the 68 who had begun the voyage. As for the others, who had gone off in single rafts, they were never heard of again.

Captain Phillips occupied his time on the trip to Brisbane, trying to discover what had gone wrong with discipline aboard his ship. The navigator was called to his cabin and questioned about his reasons for leaving the bridge at the time of the attack. Captain Phillips apologized to him for misjudging him, but then on reflection, decided he had not misjudged him at all, and wrote a letter of reprobation.

The navigator and the others reproved asked for a formal investigation of the charges, but higher authority felt it best not to stir up new problems. The *Neosho* was gone, the investigation could do nothing but bring bad blood between professional line officers and naval reservists, since all the offenders were reserve officers. There was nothing to be accomplished, and the facts were dim. Actually in these early days of war such events were to be expected. So the matter was dropped. *Henley* steamed swiftly to Brisbane where the survivors of *Neosho* and *Sims* could have first class medical attention. She sighted nothing but one gasdrum raft with life preservers, and that was empty. At one point someone thought he heard shouts from the water, and the ship stopped and circled, but saw nothing. Finally it was decided that the "shouts" had been groans from the auxiliary water pump.

On May 13, Captain Phillips buried two more men, Seaman Second Class Ed M. Pelies of the *Sims* and Chief Water Tender O.V. Peterson, one of the heroes of the *Neosho*, who died of his wounds after the rescue. Next day the ship landed at New Farm Wharf and the survivors were taken off and rushed to hospital.

The Japanese were making a big thing of their "tremendous victory" at Coral Sea. Sergeant Kawakami faithfully wrote in his diary the information he had received from Radio Tokyo about the official communiqué, and he believed every word of it. Japanese crowing became louder as the days went on, and the American Navy refused to make any statements about the battle. Radio Tokyo began mocking:

ON 7 MAY, THE U.S. NAVY ANNOUNCED THE SINKING OF 17 JAPANESE WARSHIPS IN THE CORAL SEA. THE AMERICAN PEOPLE JUBILANTLY CELEBRATED THE OCCASION.

ON 8 MAY WHEN THE JAPANESE COMMUNIQUE WAS ISSUED ON THE TRUE OUTCOME OF THIS BATTLE, AMERICAN OFFICIALS STATED, "WE MUST NOT BELIEVE JAPANESE CLAIMS, BUT AT THE SAME TIME WE MUST NOT GET OVERCONFIDENT."

ON 9 MAY, SECRETARY KNOX STATED THAT AS YET THERE WAS NO DETAILED INFORMATION ON THE OUTCOME OF THE BATTLE, BUT AMERICANS SHOULD REFRAIN FROM MAKING COMMENTS ON THE SEA BATTLE. HE ALSO SAID THAT THE AMERICAN PEOPLE SHOULD NOT ENTERTAIN TOO MUCH OPTIMISM. SINCE THEN, THE TONE OF AMERICAN PROPAGANDA CHANGED.

THE NEW YORK *TIMES* COMMENTED, "THE CORAL SEA BATTLE DECIDED THE FATE OF AUSTRALIA AND INDIA, ETC."

WHY SUCH A SUDDEN CHANGE IN THE TONE OF AMERICAN PROPAGANDA? THEY ARE OBLIGED TO ADMIT THE MISERABLE DEFEAT OF THE AMERICAN NAVY.

Next day, Admiral Sankichi Takahashi, the retired commander in chief of the combined fleet, told a correspondent of Asahi Shimbun that the formidable power of the Japanese fleet was amazing to him. The British and American navies simply could not stand up, he said, and the sinking of the *Prince of Wales* and *Repulse* off Singapore had shown it. The Americans had claimed that the Japanese smashed Pearl Harbor only because they staged a sneak attack, but

Coral Sea had proved that the Americans were no match for the Japanese.

Radio Tokyo now began a furious campaign to turn Australians against the war and against their allies, who had "let them down so badly" by being defeated at Coral Sea.

There is only one way left for Australia—total annihilation by Japanese force, if she chooses to remain under British imperialistic rule. Time is running short, but Australia may still right herself.

Yet behind the calm facade, Admiral Yamamoto was very much concerned. He was truly worried about the vast increase in activity of the American fleet in the South Pacific in the past few weeks, and he was determined to wipe out that fleet. That would, perhaps, cause the Americans to sue for peace. Admiral Yamamoto knew America well, and he knew that industrially the United States had a capacity to produce several new navies, given time. Japan had no time; she had strained herself to the utmost to produce the navy that existed on December 7. She must have a period of quiet in order to assemble the materials and men to build more of her war machine. She could not assimiliate all she had conquered overnight. If the Americans were to go on the attack, it would mean the end of the Japanese empire. So the Americans must be stopped before they could really get started; their morale must be crushed, as it had most certainly not been at Coral Sea. And the American people must be convinced that the Japanese could not be defeated. Thus he would strike at Midway, and he knew that such a strike at the heartline of the American navy would bring the admirals out in strength to fight. So he would take the Japanese fleet to Midway, and he would crush the American fleet that he knew was just now inferior to his own. Hopefully, then, he could dictate the terms of peace, and Japan would have her respite.

All this was the result of what Nimitz, Halsey, Fletcher, and Fitch had been doing in recent weeks, and the culminating blow to Yamamoto was the failure of Admiral Takagi to strike the decisive blow at Coral Sea.

In Washington, Admiral King felt much the same way about Admiral Fletcher's performance. He had really been hoping for a decisive victory at Coral Sea, and felt that Fletcher had fiddled around when he should have been hitting the Japanese hard. He took no stock in the arguments about fuel tanks and fuelling and gunsights and shortage of fighter planes. He wanted results, and he wanted men who would get those results with the material at hand.

As Fletcher read his orders and headed for Pearl Harbor as fast as he could go, Admiral King let Admiral Nimitz know how he felt, and Nimitz made ready to question Fletcher about his lack of aggressiveness. When Fletcher arrived at Pearl Harbor, his first meeting would be with Nimitz, and he would have a complete going over. But Nimitz, a much more kindly man than King, felt that Fletcher had done well on the whole, and he proposed to save him if he could. He would save him for the moment. *Yorktown* would go into drydock where a six-month repair job would be accomplished in three days, and Fletcher, as senior officer, would lead the fleet into battle at Midway. But in that battle, his deficiencies and bad luck would cause him to lose *Yorktown* and turn the battle over to a young admiral named Raymond Spruance, who would get full credit for the victory the inferior American force achieved over the Japanese juggernaut. Like Takagi, Admiral Fletcher would be eclipsed.

So the battle of Coral Sea was ended, and military historians would argue about it, in years to come, but would conclude that it was a tactical Japanese victory, as Tokyo claimed, but a strategic American victory. For Coral Sea meant the end of Japanese expansion southward. The Imperial forces would not again threaten Australia and New Zealand. The perimeter was not established.

The Imperial plan called for invasion of New Caledonia and Fiji in July, and carrier strikes against Australia, preliminary to invasion, in August. But the occupation of Port Moresby and the knockout of Australian air power there was a necessary preliminary for all this, and that occupation had been foiled by the Americans at Coral Sea. It would never come about. In a few weeks the Americans would land on Guadalcanal, and after months of attrition warfare the Japanese would be driven out of the Solomon Islands. So there would be no more bases, no more expansion, no more victories for Japan. From this point on, the Japanese were marching down the road of defeat. That was the significance of Coral Sea. In a very few months Sergeant Kawakami would be relieved of his onerous duties as a prison camp guard and sent to fight in battle, as a soldier should. He would ship to Rabaul, and then he would go to Guadalcanal. One November day, after one of the Banzai charges against the Marines, Americans searching the battlefield for survivors would come upon Sergeant Kawakami's body, and would take from it his diary, the journal of his hopes and fears, and the record of his army life. They would see, in leafing through the pages, how all had turned about for Sergeant Kawakami just after the Battle of the Coral Sea.

Notes

The Battle of the Coral Sea is based almost entirely on official documents of the U.S. and Japanese Navies, diaries and narratives in the possession of the U.S. Navy's Department of Naval History, Classified Archives. Dr. Dean Allard of this division was helpful as he has been over many years on many books. Mrs. Kathy Lloyd, archivist in charge of the World War II material, was also helpful as usual in finding materials.

1. The diary of the Japanese non-commissioned officer, used in the prologue and elsewhere, is from a captured Japanese document. The diary was taken from a body on Guadalcanal, and the translation is in the possession of the naval archives. The story of Lieutenant Sato and his detachment and their activity on New Britian island is from another captured Japanese document; in the files of the naval history division—a report by Sato on his activity. The story of Japanese fleet movements is from Japanese documents and from Samuel Eliot Morison's History of U.S. Naval Operations in World War II, volume III. The characterization of various admirals comes from brief biographies of these admirals in the hands of the naval history division, apparently prepared by U.S. naval attachés in Japan before World War II.

Chapter One

The discussion of intelligence is from the naval history files. My own *How They Won the War in the Pacific: Nimitz and His Admirals* (Weybright and Talley, 1970), included much of this material, and I used it again here, briefly. The specific Japanese layouts were described in an appendage to Admiral Fletcher's Operational Orders that led to the battle of the Coral Sea. I used the copy attached to Destroyer *Anderson*'s action report of May 8, 1942.

Chapter Two

The discussion of Japanese intentions and ideas is from a compendium of Japanese interviews for the US Strategic Bombing Survey, and the action reports of various units involved in the Battle of the Coral Sea. The reference to Nimitz and King in San Francisco is from *How They Won the War in the Pacific*. The biography of Fletcher is from the naval files. The story of the Tulagi action comes from the Action Report of Task Force 17, and specific detail from the action report of *Yorktown* for May 4, 1942.

Chapter Three

The Tulagi attack is from the report of Task Force 17, and the Japanese side from captured Japanese document No 48427, a report of Japanese operations in the southeast area in 1942. Part of the Japanese activity is covered in Morison, also. The story of the rescue of the two pilots is from the action report of *Hammann*, May 4, 1942.

Chapter Four

The story of the Japanese at Bandoeng is from the captured diary. The story of Admiral Fletcher's activity is from his action report as commander of Task Force 17, for the period May 4-8, 1942. The story of the Japanese is from various captured Japanese documents of the 25th Air Flotilla and the Port Moresby force.

Chapter Five

The story of *Neosho and Sims* is from the survivors' report written by Chief Petty Officer R. J. Dicken, and the action report and war diary of *Neosho* kept by Captain Phillips, and in the possession of the naval archives.

Chapter Six

The tale of action of May 7 is from the various action reports of units of Task Force 17, in the naval history archives. The tale of the sinking of *Shoho* is from survivors as told in captured documents, and later in interviews after the war with the Strategic Bombing Survey. The account of Lieutenant Commander Dixon's famous remark is from Morison.

Chapter Seven

Crace's Chase is described by his own action report included in the papers of the Task force, and by *Chi-*

cago's. The tale of the bombing of *Walke* by U.S. B-17s is from the narrative of Chief Fire Controlman R.F. Spearman, in the naval history files.

Chapter Eight

The story of *Neosho* again is from the documents collected in the *Neosho*'s file in the naval history division.

Chapter Nine

The diary of the Japanese non-commissioned officer is the basis for the first page of this chapter. The story of Lieutenant Williams is from his own narrative in the naval history files. The Takagi report is from the war diaries of various Japanese vessels concerned in the fight, taken after the end of the war and in the naval history files. The story of the strike on *Shokaku* is from the various action reports of air units and the ships.

Chapter Ten

The story of the Japanese attack on the American task force is largely from the files of Task Force 17.

Chapter Eleven

The stories of the attack as seen from the support ships is from the action reports of the various ships.

Chapter Twelve

This chapter comes from the action reports of Admiral Fitch and Captain Sherman and Commander Seligman, from the Williams narrative, and from Chaplain Markle's narrative, and Lieutenant Roach's narrative in the naval history files.

Chapter Thirteen

The *Neosho* file is the basis for this chapter.

Chapter Fourteen

The files of Task Force 17, the various narratives already cited, and Stanley Johnston's *Queen of the Flattops*, the story of *Lexington*, are the sources of this chapter. The Japanese activity and point of view come from various captured documents of the ships involved, interviews of the USSBS, and Morison.

Chapter Fifteen

The *Neosho* story is from the *Neosho* file.

Chapter Sixteen

The story of *Lexington*'s sinking is from various action reports. Although Stanley Johnston had the ship going down in full view, that was editorial license in a time of war. The fact was that she was hidden and nobody saw her go down.

If I seem harsh about the American naval torpedoes, I am not nearly so harsh about them as various officers, particularly submarine captains, were at the time. The whole torpedo story of the American peacetime navy was simply a fiasco.

Chapter Seventeen

The *Neosho* story is from the *Neosho* file.

Chapter Eighteen

The various elements here were my own study of Nimitz and his command, Fletcher's action report, and various Japanese official and unofficial recollections of the period, including Masanori Ito's *The End of the Imperial Japanese Navy*. The story of Commander DeWitt and *Minneapolis* is from the Minneapolis action report and Stanley Johnston's book.

Chapter Nineteen

The story of *Neosho* is from the *Neosho* file.

Chapter Twenty

The same.

Chapter Twenty-one

The various reports from Tokyo and the U.S. are from newspaper files and the intelligence reports of

Radio Tokyo intercepts of the period. The story of Nimitz is from my earlier investigations as written in *How They Won the War in the Pacific*. The *Henley* and *Neosho* reports are the basis for this story.

Bibliographical Note

Except for the always vital study of United States Naval Operations in World War II by Samuel Eliot Morison, this book does not depend on very many printed sources. Most of the material comes from the action reports of the various ships involved in the Battle of the Coral Sea, and certain captured Japanese documents—ships' reports, diaries, and the like.

It also depends on a number of interviews, most important of which was a long one with Vice Admiral Aubrey Fitch, USN Retired, conducted in his summer home in Maine in 1970. Also important were an interview, conducted that same year, with Admiral Thomas W. Kinkaid, commander of cruisers in this battle, and interviews with a number of other officers who either served in the force or were involved in critical studies of the action for the staff or for history.

Nearly all the other materials come from the Classified Archives of the United States Navy, under supervision of the Naval History Division in the Washington Navy Yard. They include:

Diary of Sergeant Kawakami of the Uchino Butai, Imperial Japanese Army
Diary of Lt. Kiyoshige Sato of Imperial Japanese Army

US Naval Intelligence report on Admiral Inouye
War Diary *Shokaku*
War Diary *Shoho*
War Diary *Zuikaku*
US Naval Intelligence Summary, New Guinea Area, Spring 1942
War Diary CINCPAC Spring 1942
Action Report Task Force 17
Various action summaries, Battle of the Coral Sea, from captured Japanese documents and interviews U.S. Strategic Bombing Survey.
Action Reports, Torpedo Squadron 5, Fighter 5, Bombing 5
Action Reports *Yorktown*
Action reports *Lexington*
Action report *Neosho*
Survivors Report *Sims*
Action report *Hammann*
Action report *Perkins*
Reports, 25th Japanese Air Flotilla
Action Report. HMAS *Australia*
Action Report HMAS *Hobart*
Action Report *Chicago*
Action Report *Farragut*
Action Report *Walke*
War Diary *Neosho*
Personal Narrative Lt. C. M. Williams
Action Reports, *Lexington* Air Group
Action reports *Portland*
Action reports *Astoria*
Action reports *Chester*
Action reports *Russell*
Action reports *Minneapolis*
Action reports *New Orleans*
Action reports *Morris*
Action reports *Anderson*

Action reports *Phelps*
Action reports *Dewey*
Personal Narrative Chaplain G.L. Markle
Personal Narrative Lt. J.F. Roach, Medical Officer
Action report *Monaghan*, May 7–8, 1942
Action reports *Henley*
Radio Intercepts, May 1942 Radio Tokyo.

The remainder of the sources cited are mentioned in the chapter notes.

INDEX

253

254

255

257

Pinnacle Books proudly presents

A BICENTENNIAL CLASSICS SERIES

Starting with four great American historical novels by Bruce Lancaster, one of America's most distinguished historians.

_____TRUMPET TO ARMS An exceptionally crafted romance spun beautifully amidst the fury of the American Revolution. (PB-887, 1.75)
"Explosive in style . . . _Trumpet to Arms_ is always easy to read and strikes a note as stirring as a call to battle."
—*The Boston Globe*

_____THE SECRET ROAD A fascinating, yet little known account of the exploits of Washington's Secret Service. A gripping story of America's first espionage unit. (PB-889, 1.75)
"A veteran craftsman at the top of his form."
—*The New York Times*

_____PHANTOM FORTRESS A masterful treatment of the career of General Francis Marion, known to history as "The Swamp Fox." (PB-905, 1.75)
"History that is good and galloping, for competent scholarship underlies the romantic story."
—*New York Herald Tribune*

_____BLIND JOURNEY An absorbing tale of romance and adventure that moves from 18th-century France and its grandeur to the carnage of revolutionary America. A story no one should miss. (PB-915, 1.75)
"Romance, adventure . . . full pulsing life. Bruce Lancaster's best."
—*The Boston Herald*

Check which books you want. If you can't find any of these books at your local bookstore, simply send the cover price plus 25¢ per book for postage and handling to us and we'll mail you your book(s).

PINNACLE BOOKS
275 Madison Avenue, New York, New York 10016

'A Question of Balance—
perhaps the most important question the
United States will ever answer—perhaps the
last.

Conflict between Russia and China is inevitable—
What does the United States do when *both* sides come
for help?

This is

THE CHINESE ULTIMATUM

P974 $1.95

The year is 1977. Russia and China have assembled troops on the
Mongolian border, and are fighting a "limited" war. A reunited
Germany and a bellicose Japanese military state have joined the
battle. The United States must step in, or be considered the enemies
of both. The Chinese have said their last word on the subject—
what will ours be?

"Absolutely gripping, I couldn't put it down."
—Rowland Evans, syndicated political columnist
"This novel is too incredibly real . . . and damnably possible!"
—an anonymous State Department official
